LET'S REASON TOGETHER

...Youths' A-Z

BOOK 2

LET'S REASON TOGETHER
...Youths' A-Z
BOOK 2

© *Oluwakemi. O. Ola - Ojo 2010*

Let's Reason Together
...Youths' A-Z
Book 2

Published by Protokos Publishers, United Kingdom
© 2010 by Oluwakemi Ola-Ojo

ISBN – 978-0-9557898-9-2

ALL RIGHTS RESERVED
No part of this publication may be reproduced, stored in a retrieval system, or transmitted in any form or by any means without prior permission of the Publishers.

Protokos Publishers 2010
P.O. Box 48424
SE15 2YL, London, United Kingdom.

'Let's Reason Together ...Youths' A-Z

DEDICATION

This book is dedicated to Youths and Young People all over the world.

'Let's Reason Together ...Youths' A-Z

1. REMEMBER [earnestly] also your Creator [that you are not your own, but His property now] in the days of your youth, before the evil days come or the years draw near when you will say [of physical pleasures], I have no enjoyment in them--
2. Before the sun and the light and the moon and the stars are darkened [sight is impaired], and the clouds [of depression] return after the rain [of tears];
3. In the day when the keepers of the house [the hands and the arms] tremble, and the strong men [the feet and the knees] bow themselves, and the grinders [the molar teeth] cease because they are few, and those who look out of the windows [the eyes] are darkened;
4. When the doors [the lips] are shut in the streets and the sound of the grinding [of the teeth] is low, and one rises up at the voice of a bird {and} the crowing of a cock, and all the daughters of music [the voice and the ear] are brought low;
5. Also when [the old] are afraid of danger from that which is high, and fears are in the way, and the almond tree [their white hair] blooms, and the grasshopper [a little thing] is a burden, and desire {and} appetite fail, because man goes to his everlasting home and the mourners go about the streets {or} marketplaces.
6. [Remember your Creator earnestly now] before the silver cord [of life] is snapped apart, or the golden bowl is broken, or the pitcher is broken at the fountain, or the wheel broken at the cistern [and the whole circulatory system of the blood ceases to function];

7. Then shall the dust *[out of which God made man's body]* return to the earth as it was, and the spirit shall return to God Who gave it.

8. **Vapor of vapors {and} futility of futilities, says the Preacher. All is futility** *(emptiness, falsity, vainglory, and transitoriness)!*

9. And furthermore, because the Preacher was wise, he *[Solomon]* still taught the people knowledge; and he pondered and searched out and set in order many proverbs.

10. The Preacher sought acceptable words, even to write down rightly words of truth {or} correct sentiment.

11. The words of the wise are like prodding goads, and firmly fixed *[in the mind]* like nails are the collected sayings which are given *[as proceeding]* from one Shepherd.

12. But about going further *[than the words given by one Shepherd]*, my son, be warned. Of making many books there is no end *[so do not believe everything you read]*, and much study is a weariness of the flesh.

13. **All has been heard; the end of the matter is: Fear God *[revere and worship Him, knowing that He is]* and keep His commandments, for this is the whole of man *[the full, original purpose of his creation, the object of God's providence, the root of character, the foundation of all happiness, the adjustment to all inharmonious circumstances and conditions under the sun]* {and} the whole [duty] for every man.**

14. **For God shall bring every work into judgment, with every secret thing, whether it is good or evil.**

Ecclesiastes 12:1-14

Acknowledgment

God is to be praised for the insight and anointing He blessed me with in writing this book.

I am grateful to God for my family and friends whose understanding and cooperation have blessed my life and writing.

I am very grateful to Pastor Imo Ihezie for writing the foreword to Book 2 of **Let's reason together-Youth's A-Z.** His constant asking and encouragement has positively inspired me to complete this project.

Thanks to Mrs Bolanle Sogunro who edited this book inspite of her other commitments.

Thanks to all who found time to read and comment on this book for their invaluable comments and encouragements.

And finally, I want to thank Protokos Publishers for the excellent work they have done and for making my dreams come true in publishing and marketing my books.

FOREWORD

Youth ministry is one vital aspect of ministry we cannot afford to toy with. Thank God there is hardly any Christian that disagrees with this vital truth. Sad to say, apart from agreeing with the fact that this ministry is very important, not much has been done to help our youths, teenagers inclusive to be the best that they can be for God. I therefore, thank God for the likes of Oluwakemi Ola- Ojo, who not only sees the need for effective youth's ministry, but has taken a step further by putting this wonderful book together for youths around the world.

Each of the twenty six (26) lessons in this book has plenty to offer as we strive to apply them in helping our youths mould their future, personality and character. I strongly recommend this book to families, church youths departments and, of course, the independent youth or teen's ministry worker.

I have no doubt in my mind that it will meet a great need in the lives of youth's ministry workers who are always faced with the challenge of sourcing for good teaching and resource materials for equipping their youths.

Pastor Imo Ihezie
President Teenager's Outreach Ministries (TOM)
TOM HOUSE
Plot 85, Ladi Kwali Extension Layout Kwali,
FCT Abuja, Nigeria

'Let's Reason Together ...Youths' A-Z

CONTENTS *Page*

Dedication v
Acknowledgement viii
Foreword ix
Content xi
Introduction xv
Strategy For Use xviii
A: Anger 23
B: Betrayal 33
C: Contentment 45
D: Drugs 55
E: Examination 67
F: Faith 77
G: Growth 87
H: Homosexuality 97
I: Ignorance 109
J: Jealousy 117
K: Kindness 125
L: Lawful 133
M: Money 143
N: Name 153

O:	Obedience	161
P:	Praise	171
Q:	Quiet time	181
R:	Rejection	191
S:	Sex	203
T:	Temptations	223
U:	Unbelief	233
V:	Vision	241
W:	Words	251
X:	X-ray	259
Y:	Youth	269
Z:	Zeal	279

Summary 285
Poems 288
Opportunity to Become a Christian 302
Other Books 304
Useful Links 310

'Let's Reason Together ...Youths' A-Z

BOOK 1

CONTENTS *Page*

Dedication	v
Acknowledgement	viii
Foreword	ix
Content	x
Introduction	xiv
Strategy for Use	xvi

A:	Attitude	21
B:	Bible	37
C:	Choices	47
D:	Dreams	63
E:	Endurance	73
F:	Forgiveness	83
G:	Giving	93
H:	Humility	105
I:	Integrity	113
J:	Justice	121
K:	Knowledge	133
L:	Love	145
M:	Miracles	159
N:	Networking	169
O:	Oath	179

P:	Presentation	189
Q:	Quest	199
R:	Respect	209
S:	Sin	219
T:	Truth	233
U:	Unity	247
V:	Vacation	257
W:	Wealth	265
X:	Xenophobic	275
Y:	Yoke	283
Z:	Zest	291

Summary 297
Opportunity to Become a Christian 300
Other Books 302
Useful Links 312

Introduction to Book 2

Welcome to **Let's Reason Together: Youths' A-Z (Book 2)** where we shall continue our discussion on issues relating to teenagers' and youths' lives from Biblical and other perspectives.

Like the **Book 1**, we have derived a topic from each of the 26 alphabets of the English language with each letter of the alphabet representing another topic for discussion, but different from the topics in Book 1.

For example, while the letter "A" stands for Attitude in Book 1, the same letter of the alphabet stands for Anger in Book 2. It therefore does not really matter which of the books you choose to study first, whether Book 2 or Book 1, the important thing is for you to have an opportunity of dialoguing with God, which these books present and, to seek Godly counsel with the hope of getting to a desired and glorious end.

Many teenagers and youths have accused the older generation of not listening or dialoguing with them on life's current and significant issues. This book seeks to remedy that anomaly as you are able to use it as a personal guide or in a group or church or family setting. The title, Lets' Reason Together is taken from Isaiah 1:18 which says *"Come now, let us reason together, says the Lord. Though your sins are like scarlet, they shall be as white as snow; though they are red as crimson, they shall be like wool."*

Reliable and open communication permits progress. It really does not matter how good or horrible your past might have been, coming just as you are to God; dialoguing with Him and, walking within His set ways can turn things around for you for the best. Each one of us needs to come to the realization of where we are; both in the physical and spiritual realms, take time to think and dialogue, have a case or situation review with God and, accept God's offer of a fresh beginning if need be.

Come brother, come sister, let's be open, let's reason together on issues and subjects that are peculiar to us, let's be willing to positively change for the best, let's prayerfully and carefully treasure this one life that we all have been given for as long as we have it.

"Now to him who is able to establish you by my gospel and the proclamation of Jesus Christ, according to the revelation of the mystery hidden for long ages past, but now revealed and made known through the prophetic writings by the command of the

eternal God, so that all nations might believe and obey him - to the only wise God be glory forever through Jesus Christ! Amen" [*Romans 16:25-27 NIV*].

STRATEGY FOR USE

Someone amongst the teenagers or youth is chosen to be the moderator; he/she should have read the information/text ahead of the discussions, be prepared for leading, and is allowed to add any relevant local information as the list has not been exhausted. He/she moderates by asking the questions as outlined in this book but may add other relevant questions. Members of the group are equally encouraged to participate/contribute to the discussion. The adult supervising the group gives an altar call at the end of the discussions, and appropriate time is spent counselling those who may so require afterwards.

It is good to allow group members to act as moderator in turns. The moderator and the supervising adult for the day should also have read the manuscript ahead of the meeting.

There is more to each topic chosen per alphabet. There is need to make the discussion as relevant to the community/people as much as it is practicable therefore there should be flexibility in the discussions.

A key phrase/scripture is given to help each teenager or youth to remember what the alphabet stands for and it is my prayers that these will be committed into memory for present and future needs/guidance.

As a good gesture, I have included some write-up on some additional alphabets with different topics on our website which is free for you. Do please tell your friends about the series and how it has helped you and we love to hear from you too. Write to us or visit www.protokospublishers.com and leave us your comments. God bless you real good.

ANGER

"Anger is one letter short of danger."

"Do not be quick in spirit to be angry {or} vexed, for anger {and} vexation lodge in the bosom of fools."
[Ecclesiastes 7:9].

Question For Consideration/Discussion:
1. What is anger?
2. When do people get angry?
3. Why do people get angry?
4. A hungry man is an angry man. What does this mean?
5. Anger and danger: how are they related?
6. Examples of angry people in the Bible.
7. Effects of anger.
8. Be angry but sin not. How?
9. How to deal with anger.
10. How to deal with an angry person.

What is Anger?

Anger is an emotion, which portrays annoyance, irritation, fury, rage, provocation, displeasure, antagonism, aggravation, infuriation, hatred, bitterness, resentment or exasperation. If not controlled it will, like any other emotion, control the person. Anger is one alphabet short of danger.

When do people get Angry?

Anytime and any where.

Why do people get Angry?

When they feel cheated, when they have lost someone or something precious to them e.g. a job, good health, time, money or wealth or when things don't go according to previous plans; when they cannot have their way; being treated unfairly, loss of freedom for those in institutions or prison. Any significant loss or threat to loosing something or someone precious can cause anger. Anger could also be the reaction secondary to corrupt or wicked practices or perceived wrong in the community/society e.g. injustice, murder, child abuse etc.

ANGER

A hungry man is an Angry man – what does this mean?

A hungry person is in need of food to fill his or her stomach and is therefore vulnerable to anger at the slightest provocation. Please avoid any debate or quarrel with a hungry person.

Anger and danger: how are they related?

A person with an uncontrolled anger will become dangerous to him/herself and others around. Anger distorts thinking as it magnifies problems or situations to be many times more serious than they really are. For example, a person with an uncontrolled anger behind the steering wheel of a vehicle is an accident waiting to happen if care is not taken.

Examples of angry people in the Bible –
1. Cain *(Genesis 4:1-16)*.
2. Levi and Simeon *(Genesis 34: 1-31; 49: 5-7)*.
3. Moses *(Exodus 2:10-16, 3; 32:15–20; 34; Numbers 20:1-12)*.
 ** *Ironically Moses was a descendant of Levi. See Genesis 49:4-7.*
4. Absalom *(2 Samuel 13: 1-31)*.
5. Joab *(2 Samuel 2:11-32; 3: 6-39; 1 Kings 2:5-6)*.

Study the scriptural references and discuss each of the examples in terms of the incident(s) that caused the anger and the results or consequences of the anger.

Effects of Anger

A burst of uncontrolled anger can cause people to do things they will later regret e.g. destroy life and, or property as often seen in road rage.

Prolonged uncontrolled anger could result in many medical conditions ranging from headache, lack of sleep, inability to eat, palpitation, high blood pressure and stroke to other dangerous disease. It may get a person into prison for acts like assault, murder and damages to other people's life and property. Spiritually, uncontrolled or prolonged anger is a sin that will cause a loss of relationship between that person and God.

Be Angry and not sin. How?

The anger must be for the right reasons e.g. injustice, child abuse etc. It must propel us to improve the situation making us angry e.g. defending the poor in cases of injustice, giving support in cash and kind to the abused etc. God allows us to be angry but to a limit. We must learn to put our anger under control. Let not the sun go down upon your wrath *(Ephesians 4:26)*.

How to deal with Anger

1. Recognise and admit it to yourself and God.
2. Identify the root or cause of your anger. If possible relocate from its source.
3. Jesus said the thief i.e satan has come to kill, steal and destroy but that He has come to give us abundant life *(John 10:10)*. As every reasonable person will try and save their belongings from the thief, you need to save your life, testimony, health and wealth from the destructive effects of anger.
4. Minimal damage is done if you deal quickly with your anger. Take a walk, not drive, to help you get rid of the extra adrenaline in you. This will also give you time to think more clearly and deal with the cause of your anger rationally.
5. There are things that are not within your control so accept them and don't let such wind you up e.g. a delayed post, a sick friend or teacher etc.
6. Anger, like any other attitude can be contagious, please avoid the company of irritable and angry people lest you subconsciously begin to act like them.

7. Do not let the sun go down with you still being angry. It is not worth it.

How to deal with an Angry person

- Acknowledge that they are angry.
- Listen to the angry person but do not add more fuel to the anger nor shush the person.
- If you can, identify why they are angry.
- Show the person godly unconditioned love.
- Give help, assistance and support to the angry person if they will allow you.
- When they have cooled down, which may not be immediately, review the cause of the anger with the person and see if you can help to make life easier and more pleasant for the person by offering help within your means if needed. E.g. if the person is angry due to hunger, you could share your food with him/her.

Exercise

- ◈ Identify times that you have been angry.
- ◈ Determine the cause of the anger.
- ◈ Evaluate what your angry response cost or is costing you.
- ◈ Given that you knew then what you know now about the situation, would you have been that angry?
- ◈ What steps have you taken or will you take in controlling anger and its effects in your life?

Prayer Points

Lord, please deliver me from all forms of ungodly anger.

'Be not hasty in thy spirit to be angry: for anger resteth in the bosom. of fools' Ecclesiastes 7:9.

Father, please help me not to be a fool.

Lord, please help me to bring a positive change to the cause of my anger.

'Let's Reason Together ...Youths' A-Z

MY PERSONAL NOTES

BETRAYAL

"Betrayal is wickedness."

"But, behold, the hand of him who is now engaged in betraying Me is with Me on the table"
[Luke 22:21]

Questions For Consideration/Discussion:
1. What is betrayal, backstabbing or grassing?
2. Who is a betrayer?
3. Why do people betray or backstab others?
4. Examples of betrayal / backstabbing in the Bible.
5. How to deal with betrayal / backstabbing.
6. Can I trust anyone again?
7. How to deal with someone who has been betrayed or backstabbed.
8. What to do if you have betrayed or backstabbed anyone.

What is the Betrayal?

It involves being unfaithful, disloyal, deceitful, or fraudulent to someone who trusts you. This might mean disclosing the secret that a person has kept with you, using information about that person behind them to destroy them or cause them some trouble.

Who is a Betrayer?

A betrayer is double-faced, usually heartless and wicked. Betrayers are usually close to a person they want to betray but with a hidden agenda whilst they pretend to love, cherish, support and protect the one they eventually will betray. They take time to study the person they want to betray and often cunningly get to know the secret of that person. They then use that information against the person or hand it over to others to use against him or her. Modern examples are the 'kiss and tell' stories.

Why do people Betray others?

People betray others mostly to make money or gain a prominent position. Betrayal could also be due to jealousy or to destroy the person physically, emotionally, socially, economically, financially etc.

Examples of betrayal / backstabbing in the Bible –
1. Joseph *(Genesis 37:1-38).*
2. Samson *(Judges 14:1-20; 15: 1-7; 16: 4-31).*
3. Jesus Christ *(Matthew 26:14-16; 27; 28).*

Study the scriptural references and discuss each of the examples in terms of the incident(s) that caused the betrayal and the results or consequences of the betrayal.

Effects of Betrayal

To be betrayed could be exceedingly painful. It could bring deep hurt, anger, hatred, frustration, bitterness and hopelessness. It certainly is a trying and turbulent time. When you have been backstabbed, it is normal to have all of the above or more feelings including guilt for allowing that person(s) near you in the first place. So what do you do?

How to deal with betrayal/backstabbing:

Please tell God exactly how you feel. He can handle all your volcanic emotional eruptions. Avoid bitterness or its seed.

Recognise that God allowed the betrayal for a purpose that might not be immediately apparent but which will invariably be made manifest. As long as you remain in the Lord, He will make all things including the betrayal to work for your good *(Romans 8:28)*. Joseph for example later became the first Prime Minister in Egypt, a position he could not have attained in Canaan, thereby fulfilling the dreams God had shown him previously.

Samson killed more Philistines at his death than when he was alive. Jesus paid for our sins in full on the cross of Calvary and mankind was restored back to God, He rose from the dead never to die again and today He has a name that is above every other name in heaven, on earth and under the earth. At the mention of His name, every knee bows and all tongues confess that He is Lord. The bottom line is that God allowed the betrayal and will use it to fulfil His plan for you if you do not sin.

Can I trust anyone again?

Yes with the help of the Lord through the Holy Spirit, with maturity through that experience, with a good network support, you can and will learn to trust again with time. As you walk with God and learn to trust Him, you will realise

BETRAYAL

more that it is only with Him that your secrets can indeed be secret.

How to deal with someone who has been betrayed/ backstabbed–

- Acknowledge the situation.
- Avoid rubbing it in.
- Give them space and time to deal with it.
- Pray for them and with them if they would allow you
- Periodically encourage them.
- Avoid trying to have a close friendship with them unless /until they invite you into their personal space.
- Respect their wishes for privacy or withdrawal but pray for them.
- Pray with them if they ask you to do so.
- Show them genuine love.
- Do not apportion any blame, as you have not heard the betrayal's story.

What to do if you have betrayed or backstabbed anyone:

- Identify the underlying cause or root of the betrayal or backstabbing – e.g. are you a gossiper? Was it because you felt insecure, envious, in need, vulnerable, etc?

- What reward was given to you for betraying/backstabbing that person?
- If the roles could be reversed, how would you have felt to be betrayed by someone like you did?
- What were the consequences of your betrayal to the person you betrayed?
- Are you likely to betray other people i.e. was it a 'one off' or your routine lifestyle?
- Confess your sins to God and ask for His mercies.
- Seek Godly counsel so that this does not become a lifestyle.
- Prayerfully ask for forgiveness from the person you betrayed. Be prepared for a negative welcome.

BETRAYAL

Exercise

❖ Identify times that you or someone close to you was betrayed or you betrayed someone else.
❖ Evaluate what you think /know caused it.
❖ Evaluate the consequences of your backstabbing to that other person e.g. loss of dignity, money or friends; anger.
❖ What is the betrayal costing you?
❖ If you knew then what you know now about that person who betrayed you what could you have done to prevent the situation?
❖ How trusting are you now?
❖ Will you betray anyone again?

Prayers Points:

For the betrayal:

Lord, please forgive me for betraying/ backstabbing others (you might want to name the person(s).

Father, please help me to forgive myself for betraying others. Lord help me to be trust worthy as from now on.

BETRAYAL

For the betrayed:

Lord, please help me to forgive all my betrayals.

Father, please heal me of all the hurts and negative emotions of being betrayed.

Lord, please surround me with trustworthy people fro now on.

'Let's Reason Together ...Youths' A-Z

MY PERSONAL NOTES

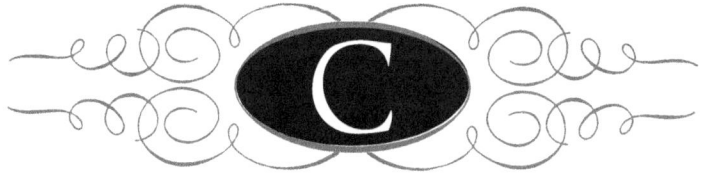

CONTENTMENT

"A contented life is a protected life."

"And it is, indeed, a source of immense profit, for godliness accompanied with contentment (that contentment which is a sense of inward sufficiency) is great {and} abundant gain."
[I Timothy 6:6].

Questions for Consideration/ Discussion:
1. What is Contentment?
2. Characteristics of a contented person.
3. With what or in which area should I be contented?
4. Why do I have to be contented?
5. Is contentment and settling for less the same?
6. Rewards of contentment.

What is Contentment?

Contentment means living within one's means happily, satisfaction, happiness, gratification, ease, fulfilment or pleasure. It does not mean to lack aspiration for a better place or position in life. It is a state of mind or attitude that is grateful to God and happy with what one has. It is having self-control. Always trying to be like the Joneses is a sign of lack of contentment. Every person has a specific life to live, and contentment helps to prevent us from trying to be like anyone else but ourselves.

Characteristics of a contented person:

A contented person will for example be happy eating a plate of rice with or without fish or meat at home if that is all that can be afforded and not be sad that he/she is not in a restaurant having a four-course meal instead. A contented person knows that with God on their side, with hard work and time, they too will one day be able to afford something better, which they would equally enjoy. A contented person is usually not jealous or envious of others, is not greedy and exercises good self-control.

CONTENTMENT

With what or in which area should I be contented?

Contentment cuts across every aspect of life. Be contented with how God made you i.e. your looks e.g. some with lovely dark skin who are not contented end up bleaching their skin thereby exposing themselves to cancer of the skin and many other medical dangers. Some who are not contented with their sex change into the opposite sex and many end up depressed. Some who are not contended with their income as a student or worker have sold their bodies and souls to the devil for money and material wealth by prostitution or other fraudulent means including stealing and armed robbery.

Why do I have to be contented?

Contentment is a good step towards integrity and self-protection. Life will at some point present short cuts, quick and easy ways of making money, getting attention and whatever else one wants, which in the end leads to nothing but destruction. A one night fling in order to get some cash for a new outfit or gadget may end in infection with a sexually transmitted incurable disease such as herpes or AIDS or an unwanted pregnancy.

Is contentment and settling for less the same?

Contentment is a situation that one involuntarily finds him or herself that can be improved upon with God's help and hard work. Whereas, settling for less means that person has the ability to do better but deliberately chooses to go for a lesser position or thing; it is often secondary to laziness, stinginess, and lack of motivation, poor self-esteem or inferiority complex. All children of God should be the best in their calling or vocation.

Rewards of contentment

It gives protection. Joseph was contented being a slave and would not commit adultery with his master's wife to get special favours. His refusal landed him in prison but later he got to the palace and on the same day of his appointment as the first Prime Minister of Egypt, he was given a wife from a high-class family *(Genesis 41:1-46)*. Daniel and his friends were contented eating beans and water as opposed to the rich food of the king and because they did not defile themselves, the Lord granted them favour, better looks, excellent examination result better than their contemporaries *(Daniel 1: 1-20)*. It is now proven that sugary drinks could make people especially children hyperactive, which is not helpful in their studies or health. Over eating is a source of obesity seen today in children and adults.

For lack of contentment, King David took Uriah's wife and God justly punished him. Someone has once said, when you take what God has not given you, God takes back what He has given you. A lack of contentment leads to all manners of evil including premature death.

Exercise:

- ❖ Are you a contented person or not? If not why not?
- ❖ Identify areas of your life where you just can't come round to being contented and the potential dangers of this to you and your family.
- ❖ Are you always comparing yourself with the Joneses and will do anything to appear like them? If so why?
- ❖ List the ways you can overcome that lack of contentment in your life.
- ❖ Seek for godly counselling. Pray and meditate on the word of God.

Prayer Points:

Lord, thank You for helping me to be a contented person or Lord, please help me to be contented and not envious of others.

Father, please help me never to settle for less than Your wish for me in life and destiny.

Lord, may I depend on You always and only, may I find true happiness in You not in the things I have or don't have.

'Let's Reason Together ...Youths' A-Z

MY PERSONAL NOTES

DRUGS

"I refuse to defile my body with drugs."

"Do you not know that your body is the temple (the very sanctuary) of the Holy Spirit Who lives within you, whom you have received [as a Gift] from God? You are not your own."
[I Corinthians 6: 19].

Question for Consideration/ Discussion:
1. What are drugs?
2. Why do people do drugs?
3. What is the effect of doing drugs?
4. How to overcome doing drugs.
5. How to help a drug addict.

What is it?

Doing drugs simply means taking non-medicated drugs or selling or distributing such. The drugs include ecstasy, cocaine, marijuana etc. These drugs may be smoked, inhaled, injected, swallowed or chewed.

Why do people do Drugs?

There are many reasons for this including:
- Peer Pressure.
- Wanting to be accepted by or belong to a group.
- Masking other pains e.g. the pain of divorce in the family, pain of perceived parental rejection, perceived peer rejection especially from the opposite sex, inferiority complex or failure, shyness or weakness.
- Wanting to show off especially in front of the opposite sex.
- Rebellion.
- Experimenting.
- Ignorance about the harmful effects of drugs on their bodies.
- Lack of the fear of God.
- Quick way of making money if you are selling it.

DRUGS

What is the effect of doing Drugs?

◈ It induces over confidence, which leads to dangerous and irrational actions.
◈ It causes a lot of misbehaviours under the influence of the drug.
◈ It causes loss of good reputation, job or salary e.g. Mutu's sack by Chelsea Football club in October 2004 for testing positive to cocaine.
◈ It is one of the reasons for keeping bad company.
◈ It is an expensive venture.
◈ It leads to involvement in many other ills e.g. lying, prostitution, stealing, killing and armed robbery.
◈ It never satisfies i.e. makes the person an addict with time.
◈ It is the cause of many terrible diseases e.g. mental health problems, liver or kidney damage or, hepatitis B & C, abscesses in the favourite spots of the injections, HIV&AIDS through needle sharing etc.
◈ It may cause the death of the user.
◈ The user many times do not get to deal with the cause for their doing drugs.

How to overcome doing Drugs.

The following has not been arranged in no particular order of importance:

- Be convinced that it is against God's will for you
- Identify the root cause of your doing drugs and deal with it.
- Confess your sins to God, ask Him to forgive you and help you.
- Depend on the Holy Spirit to help you overcome this habit.
- Spend quality time reading the Bible, studying and meditating on its contents.
- Identify places, situations and people that encourage you to do drugs.
- Avoid such places, situations and people.
- Choose a mentor who can correct and encourage you i.e. be accountable to someone e.g. your youth pastor or counsellor – you will need to open up to this mentor or counsellor so they can know where and how to help you.
- Ask God to give you a new set of godly friends.
- Get involved in the Church and youth dedicated activities.
- Seek for medical help – it is urgent and very necessary.

How to help a drug addict that seeks for your help:

- Do not judge rather identify the root cause of the person's problem and deal with it.
- Love him/her just as Jesus does.
- Pray for and with the person.
- Be careful that you are not dragged into doing drugs yourself or into the gang of those who do.
- Make sure you are trained in handling this or get a trained person/ counsellor/ Pastor that you can work along with in reaching out to this person. *(A young reporter decided to report on what went on in the drug world in one of the African nations. His colleagues and others warned him against such a venture but he refused. In the end he found himself using some of the drugs and became mentally deranged. Rather than endangering your life by covering up for your friend or trying to help if you have not been trained to do so, please refer them to the appropriate authority who may be a parent, teacher, doctor, or drug rehabilitation specialist.)*

EXERCISE:

- ❖ Have you done drugs before or are you doing now? If so, why?
- ❖ What is the drug you are doing costing you?
- ❖ Do you really want to quit doing drugs?
- ❖ What steps are you taking towards quitting?
- ❖ Who have you told the truth and sought help from?
- ❖ Have you seen a medical doctor for this? If not why not?

PRAYER POINTS:

Lord, please forgive me for all the ways I have defiled my body.

Father, please cleanse and heal me from all the defilement I have expose my body to.

Lord, please help me to keep away from all negative pressures that might want to lure me back into taking or doing unprescribed drugs from now in Jesus name.

DRUGS

SOME DRUG ADDICTION HELP LINES IN THE UK:

Croydon Drug Project – Tel. Number 0208 291 1414
Off Record Tel. Number 0208 251 0251

The Shepherd's Ministries
Tel/Fax: +44 208 698 7222
Email: info@theshepherdsministries.org
Website: www.theshepherdsministries.org

www.addictionadvisor.co.uk/drugs
Tel Number /0845 370 0102

Your local Social Services help line should be able to direct you appropriately.

IN NIGERIA:

Children's Evangelism Ministry Inc
P.O. Box 4480
Ilorin, Kwara State,
Nigeria.
Tel: +234 31 222199
E-mail: cem@ilorin.skannet.com

DRUGS

Teenagers' Outreach Ministries
Tel: +234 80370 44195
www.teenagersoutreachministries.Org

IN USA:
www.eCounseling.com
Tel Number: 1-866-268-6735

Make a contact today if you need help or someone you know or love does. You are only a phone call / contact away to your drug addiction release.

'Let's Reason Together ...Youths' A-Z

MY PERSONAL NOTES

EXAMINATION

"Examination is the pathway to promotion."

"Examine me, O Lord, and prove me; test my heart and my mind."
[Psalm 26:2].

Question for consideration/discussion:
1. What is an examination?
2. Who is being examined?
3. Why do we need to do any examinations?
4. How to prepare for any examination.
5. Examination and promotion how are they related?
6. Is failure final?

What is an examination?

It is a form of assessment, oral, or written test, an inspection, a scrutiny or an analysis of a thing, knowledge or person.

Who is being examined?

Every person on earth goes through one form of examination or the other. When a baby is born, usually after the initial cry under normal circumstances, the attending midwife or doctor will do a physical examination to test the baby's fitness. After this the baby is still re-assessed at different times and ages by a paediatrician or nurse. In school, there are also academic tests and examinations to do.

As it is in the physical realm so it is in the spiritual realm. Every one of us gets tested at certain times in life by God to promote us and by the devil who tests *(tempts)* us to make us fall or deny God.

Why do we need to do any examinations?

An examination is necessary to:
- assess the worth of a thing,
- bring out what is in a person,

EXAMINATION

- check if the person has matured or mastered a point / lesson
- bring about promotion if the person has passed
- or direct the person to areas of life that he/she needs to work on if the person has failed.

How to prepare for any examination

- ❖ Accept the fact that examinations are a common life occurrence.
- ❖ Put God first in all things and ask Him to help you
- ❖ Avoid fearing examination as it is your pathway to promotion.
- ❖ Be determined not to defile yourself with things/activities that can damage you, endanger your life, jeopardise your destiny or destroy your testimony *(e.g. premarital sex; selling your body or property in exchange for passing the test; alcohol and drug abuse; occult practices; cheating in the examination room; buying examination papers; laziness; absence from lectures for any reason except on health grounds etc).*
- ❖ Know yourself and plan for your examination from the first day of your course, for the examination will surely come. Some read and study daily so that they are not under pressure at the exam time, while others do better if they subject themselves to a lot of pressure just before

the examination. Timothy 3:15.
- ❖ Be diligent in your studies. Be prepared for the examination; lack of understanding and adequate preparation is a recipe for failure.
- ❖ Keep good friends and do not be afraid of going to those with more knowledge than you to teach you i.e. have a teachable spirit.
- ❖ Be open to constructive criticism.
- ❖ A wise lady once said that **'Proper preparation prevents poor performance' (P^5)**

Examination and promotion how are they related?

As it is in the physical so it is in the spiritual realm. In most cases, without passing the required examination you cannot be promoted. Similarly, to go to the next level in the Christian faith someone said there is a demon to fight. Joseph was tested in Portiphar's house - doing God's will landed him in the prison but that eventually got him into the palace. Daniel and his friends were tested. They purposed in their heart not to defile themselves with the king's food and at the end of three years training in the palace, they did much better than the *'sons of the land'*. The king promoted Daniel and his friends *(Daniel 1:1-20)*.

EXAMINATION

Is failure final?

Failure, like in examination, is a common life experience. In most cases failure is not final; it may just mean working harder in the areas of your weaknesses. If you have failed a test or an examination, learn from your mistakes and try again. Expert's fail, wise people also fail. The prepared fail and the unprepared fail too. Men and women, boys and girls fail. The old and the young fail. Failure is not limited to race, colour, shape or size. The man who made the light bulbs that we enjoy today failed several times but he didn't give up, he kept trying and finally his breakthrough came. That you have failed that examination does not make you a failure. The righteous man falls seven times but rises up again each time *(Proverbs 24:16)*.

EXERCISE:

◈ Have you failed before? Why?
◈ What lessons did you learn from that failure?
◈ Failure to prepare is a sure way to preparing to fail – true or false? Why?
◈ Do you have any phobia for examinations/ tests? Why?
◈ What are the things that you can do to overcome this phobia?

PRAYER POINTS:

Lord, please help me to see every obstacle and examination as a stepping stone for my promotion.

Father, please help me to daily be prepared to be examined.

Lord, please take away from me every fear that might want to make me perform poorly in life and in destiny.

EXAMINATION

MY PERSONAL NOTES

FAITH

"It is impossible for me to please God without faith."

"So faith comes by hearing [what is told], and what is heard comes by the preaching [of the message that came from the lips] of Christ (the Messiah Himself)."
[Romans 10:17]

Question For Consideration/ Discussion:
1. What is faith?
2. Why do we need faith?
3. In whom or what do I need faith?
4. Rewards of having faith.
5. Faith and fear - to have or not to have?
6. Faith killers and builders.

What is faith?

Faith means belief or confidence in something or someone; trust, assurance or conviction that something will or will not happen; devotion or loyalty in /to someone or something.

Why do we need faith?

In every kingdom there is the currency of that kingdom e.g. in the U.K. the currency is pounds sterling and pence, in the USA it is dollars and cents, in Nigeria it is naira and kobo. Faith is the currency of heaven. Without money most if not all-financial transactions cannot occur in the business world today. Without faith we cannot transact any heavenly business too.

Nothing in this world gets done without faith. For example, we sit on a chair because we believe the manufacturers have produced the chair to the standard required of them such that no one falls when they sit on it. A baby cries believing that crying will bring the desired result of food, attention, change of clothes/diaper or something.

In whom or what do I need faith? We need to have faith as Christians in the Almighty, All knowing, Ever faithful, Always loving, All powerful, Ever merciful and Gracious

God. Having faith in God also means having faith in His words that He is who He says He is, He will do what He says He will do, He is able and abundantly able to keep His promises, worthy to be praised, honoured, worshipped and obeyed.

We need to have faith in ourselves that with God on our side we can do what we set out to do, be all that God has purposed for us to be, for it is written concerning us that we can do all things through Christ who strengthens us (Philippians 4:13). You and I owe ourselves love and faith. Unless you believe in yourself, it might be very difficult for others to believe in you. You need to believe that with God's greater power inside of you, you can achieve His purpose for your life.

Rewards of having faith -

Faith in God will always be rewarded. God is not looking for a mountain size faith but a mustard seed size faith. Just as a little yeast will produce great results in a big bowl of flour, so can a little faith demolish a huge mountain of obstacles or problems. A good read of Hebrews chapter 11 will reveal the ways men and women of great faith were rewarded. Today, many are still getting healed of physical, financial, emotional, spiritual problems through faith in the Lord and His unfailing word.

Faith and fear to have or not to have?

Faith and fear are not the same just as light and darkness are not the same. Fear is the opposite of faith. Someone has defined fear as an acronym for False Evidence Appearing Real. It is impossible to have the God kind of faith and fear together. If you are struggling with faith in a particular area, make sure there is no unconfessed sin in your life. Read the Bible looking for examples of people who were in situations similar to yours and how they overcame; listen to the testimonies of those around you; remember times past when God came through for you and be encouraged by all these.

Faith killers and strengtheners

Anything or anyone that wants to undermine or destroy your faith is a faith killer and anything or anyone who seeks to enhance your faith is a faith builder. *Not arranged in a particular order:*

FAITH

Faith killers	Faith Builders
Sin	Repentance (being sorry and saying sorry)
Fear	Obedience to God and His word, Yours and others' testimony of previous experiences
Ungodly companions	Godly companions
Ingratitude	Grateful attitude
Murmuring and complaining	Songs of praise and worship
Satan	Holy Spirit

EXERCISE:

❖ In who or what is your faith?
❖ What do you understand by faith?
❖ Give an example of when your faith was stretched/tested
❖ What was the effect of your faith or lack of it at that time?
❖ In what ways can your family and friends affect or influence your faith?
❖ In what ways can what you hear, see, feel, touch, taste or smell affect your faith?

PRAYER POINTS:

Lord, please help me and teach me to put my trust in You always.

Father, please remind me of Your written and spoken promises when I am tempted to doubt You.

Lord, please surround me with people who will enhance my faith in You.

FAITH

GROWTH

"I must read my Bible and pray everyday in order to grow."

" But grow in grace (undeserved favor, spiritual strength) and recognition {and} knowledge {and} understanding of our Lord and Savior Jesus Christ (the Messiah). To Him [be] glory (honor, majesty, and splendor) both now and to the day of eternity. Amen (so be it)!."
[2 Peter 3:18]

Question For Consideration/ Discussion:
1. What is growth?
2. Types of growth.
3. Why do I need to grow?
4. How can I grow?
5. Who is responsible for my growth?
6. When to stop growing?

What is growth?

Growth means expansion, increase, enlargement, development, escalation, intensification, rise, extension, and amplification.

Types of growth

Human growth can be physical, emotional, financial, spiritual, mental or intellectual. For a child to be regarded as healthy, there must be physical, and mental growth. Spiritual growth means leaving childish behaviour but maintaining childlike attitude. 'When I was a child, I talked like a child, I thought like a child, I reasoned like a child; now that I have become a man, I am done with childish ways {and} have put them aside.*(1 Corinthians 13:11).*

Why do I need to grow?

Growth shows development. It is important in order to do what is expected of you in line with your age, exposure, or experience. For instance, a baby who refuses to grow will hardly be able to walk, run or be independent.

GROWTH

How can I grow?

Growth comes physically, mentally, spiritually, financially and emotionally. To grow physically demands that you eat a balanced diet, drink enough fluids and be healthy. To grow your muscles will require regular and appropriate exercises. To grow mentally will require exercising your mind and reading good books. To grow spiritually will involve daily reading your Bible and other good Christian literature, praying, fellowshipping with other believers, sharing your testimonies, witnessing and having a better relationship with God.

Who is responsible for your growth?

To a great extent, you are responsible for your growth right from birth. If when your parents fed you as a baby, you refused to open your mouth, or refused to suck or drink or eat; what could they have done? Growth is not automatic; it requires you making some form of effort. It must be achieved deliberately. To be able to grow you need to be teachable, as well as be willing to pay the price e.g. to become a professional calls for you to study and write the necessary examinations, to become an Olympic medallist calls for discipline, dedication, good health and adequate training.

To hear God better calls for you to spend more time in reading and meditating on the word of God; many hours of praying and sometimes fasting; becoming familiar with how God speaks to you. Be willing to learn on daily basis if need be, not relenting your efforts or sitting on past glories; be observant and refuse to be stagnant. To retain what you have learnt, apply your new knowledge to real life situations where applicable and finally, be open and willing to positive change. The world is continually changing, the message may be the same but the methods over the years have not been the same for most things. Compare going on a business trip from Africa or Australia to Britain or Japan by ship with going on the same trip by air or transacting the business on the Internet without leaving your base. *(Read James 1:22 and Proverbs 4.)*

When to stop growing?

Physically there comes an age when you stop growing taller though you can still put on some weight but you cannot afford to stop growing intellectually, financially or spiritually.

GROWTH

Exercise:

❖ Identify areas of your life where you are not growing.
❖ Why are you not growing?
❖ What can you do to increase your growth in the area you identified above?
❖ What will you want God to do to help you?
❖ How will you assess your spiritual growth compared to six or twelve months ago?
❖ Identify a godly mentor who can help you in the area of your growth challenges and be honest with this person.

Prayer Points:

Lord, in Your name and by Your grace, I refuse to be a dwarf in the events of life.

Father, may I grow in You, have the favour of God and man and be healthily equipped for my purpose in life.

Lord, please help me to grow in all areas of life — physically, spiritually, financially, emotionally, educationally, socially, etc.

GROWTH

HOMOSEXUALITY

"God's ordained sexual love is between a man and a woman."

"You shall not lie with a man as with a woman; it is an abomination." [Leviticus 18:22].

Questions For Consideration/ Discussion:
1. What is it?
2. Why do people go into homosexuality?
3. Is homosexuality a sin or not?
4. Effect of homosexuality.
5. How to overcome homosexuality.
6. How to help a homosexual.

What is It?

Baillieres Nurses Dictionary (1990) defines homosexuality as sexual and emotional orientation toward persons of the same sex. Any sexual attraction and emotional orientation between two people of the same sex is homosexual behaviour. In any homosexual relationship, you will notice one of them will adopt the role of a male and the other the role of a female.

Why do people go into homosexuality?

It is not uncommon to find that males who grew up in the company of females only with no definite father figure many times grow up wanting to be a lady and vice versa. Other reasons for homosexuality are:
- Lack of love and appreciation especially from the opposite sex.
- Not finding a lover/ spouse in the opposite sex.
- Rebellion or desire to be different.
- Adventure or fun.
- Deceit of the devil.
- Effects of sexual abuse or brainwashing in childhood by a trusted adult of same sex e.g. relative, clergy, teacher.
- Lure of money and material gifts.
- Rejection by the opposite sex.

HOMOSEXUALITY

◈ Some claim it is a medical deficiency. However, no particular virus, bacteria, blood or organ deficiency has been identified to account for such behaviour or orientation. E.g. malaria is caused by mosquito bite, cold is caused by viral/ virus infection, herpes is a sexually transmitted disease caused by a particular bug or bacteria, Turner's syndrome is caused by or secondary to a genetic malformation but to the best of my knowledge, homosexuality has not been classified as due to any of the above reasons. Equally, most homosexuals choose to be or not be like that.

Is homosexuality a sin or not?

It is an abomination according to God's law irrespective of societal acceptance or propagation of it. In the Garden of Eden, God made them male and female. God gave to Adam an Eve not a Steve! *(Genesis 1:27-31, 2:18-25)*. God loves the homosexual person but hates the sin of homosexuality. Christ died for all who will accept His lordship including the repentant homosexual.

Effect of homosexuality-

This may include any or all of the following (not in a particular order):

- Rebellion against God and the Bible.
- Inability to have a meaningful relationship with the opposite sex.
- Feeling of inward dirtiness.
- Too ashamed to disclose to anyone else or seek for help.
- Embarrassing sexual accidents that may require medical or surgical intervention.
- Sexually transmitted diseases including HIV, herpes.
- Self condemnation.
- Inability to challenge abuser especially if the person is much older or respected in the family or community.
- Inability to be all that God wants for that person in that situation.
- Emotional problems including fear, depression, etc.

How to overcome homosexuality –

- Recognise it is a sin against God, confess it to Him, not trying to justify it then ask for His forgiveness and cleansing *(1 John 1:8-9)*.
- Ask for the forgiveness of those involved with you, if and where possible.
- Forgive yourself.
- Seek for Godly counsel.
- Be accountable to someone e.g. your mentor/Pastor whom you should be honest and open with.

HOMOSEXUALITY

- If your environment has encouraged you in such practices, then you may need a change of location.
- Study the Bible, asking the Holy Spirit to help your understanding. Meditate on the word and memorise the relevant scriptures to help you.
- Spend quality time praying and if need be add fasting to it.
- Be not deceived, bad company corrupts good morals.
- To every satanic suggestion, reply with the written word of God- I tell you it works!

How to help homosexual people:

a. Pray for them.
b. Pray with them if they will allow you to do so.
c. If possible find out the reason for their behaviour and address this.
d. Love and support them as God would love and support them but not their behaviour.
e. Encourage them to seek for Godly counsel.
f. As you try to help them be careful you too are not lured into such practices.

Have you experienced homosexuality or do you know someone who has? You might want to prayerfully meditate on this song written by William A. Ogden 1887:

HOMOSEXUALITY

I've a message from the Lord, hallelujah!
This message unto you I'll give,
'Tis recorded in His word, hallelujah!
It is only that you "look and live."
Refrain:
"Look and live," my brother, live,
Look to Jesus now, and live;
'Tis recorded in His word, hallelujah!
It is only that you "look and live."

I've a message full of love, hallelujah!
A message, O my friend, for you,
'Tis a message from above, hallelujah!
Jesus said it, and I know 'tis true.

Life is offered unto you, hallelujah!
Eternal life thy soul shall have,
If you'll only look to Him, hallelujah!
Look to Jesus who alone can save.

I will tell you how I came, hallelujah!
To Jesus when He made me whole—
'Twas believing on His name, hallelujah!
I trusted and He saved my soul.

Source: http://library.timelesstruths.org/music/Look_and_Live/
midi/(words, tune and music)

HOMOSEXUALITY

EXERCISE:

- What makes people to become homosexual?
- How can you recognise a homosexual?
- How can you help a homosexual know the truth about themselves and what God wants?
- Would you knowingly have a relationship with a homosexual? Why or why not?
- Can somebody be a genuinely born again Christian and be practising homosexual acts?

PRAYER POINTS:

Lord, please help me to gladly accept Your custom designed sexual configuration for my life.

Father, in Jesus name please help me to love and protect myself from the lies of the enemy.

Lord, please help me to remember Your unfailing love for me especially when others reject me.

HOMOSEXUALITY

Help lines -
http://www.gracetreecounseling.com/
http://www.counselcareconnection.org/articles/85/1/Overcoming-Homosexuality/Page1.html
http://www.ha-fs.org/

Homosexuals Anonymous Fellowship Services
281-712-2676 or, write them at
HAFS16506 FM 529 Rd - 115 Box 113
Houston, TX 77095
http://www.exodus-international.org

IN NIGERIA:
Children's Evangelism Ministry Inc
P.O. Box 4480
Ilorin, Kwara State,
Nigeria.
Tel: +234 31 222199
E-mail: cem@ilorin.skannet.com

Teenagers' Outreach Ministries
Tel: +234 80370 44195
www.teenagersoutreachministries.org

Make a contact today if you need help or someone you know or love does. You are only a phone call / contact away to your homosexuality release.

'Let's Reason Together ...Youths' A-Z

MY PERSONAL NOTES

IGNORANCE

"All ignorance gets paid for."

"Therefore My people go into captivity [to their enemies] without knowing it {and} because they have no knowledge [of God]. And their honorable men [their glory] are famished, and their common people are parched with thirst.." [Isaiah 5:13]

Questions For Consideration/ Discussion:
1. What is it?
2. What could people be ignorant of?
3. Why are people ignorant?
4. The cost of ignorance.
5. How to overcome ignorance.

What is it?

Ignorance is unawareness or lack of knowledge of something or someone.

What could people be ignorant of?

Ignorance could be unawareness about any of the following:
- Salvation that has been fully paid for.
- Healing and deliverance that have been fully paid for by Jesus Christ
- Victory over every challenge of life
- Who they are on earth – created by God in His image to
  - have dominion over all other creatures
  - be fruitful, multiply and replenish the earth (Genesis 1:26 – 31)
- Why they are on earth today – to have dominion over the earth and
  - rule over it,
  - worship and serve God,
  - preach the gospel of Jesus Christ,
  - be God's representative to all.
- Prosperity and God's wonderful provision.
- God's promise of His abiding presence.
- Breakthroughs in the world around us today.
- Every single promise in the Bible.

IGNORANCE

❖ Whatever the problem may be, the solution is available.

Why are people ignorant?

This could be due to many reasons:
❖ Laziness in searching for the required information.
❖ Searching for information in the wrong place.
❖ Searching for information from the wrong people.
❖ Limited exposure.
❖ Not asking people who have the answer or solution to the challenge.
❖ Not matching what has been heard with the word of God.
❖ Hoarding of information by people who have it.

Cost of Ignorance:

Ignorance gets paid for directly or indirectly by the ignorant person and or the community the ignorant person serves. An ignorant parent may refuse the child access to good medical care including childhood immunisations, which may make the child to be more vulnerable to certain diseases. An ignorant student is likely to fail in the examination. An ignorant person is likely going to miss golden opportunities. An ignorant leader will lead his people astray or undervalue them. Ignorance is never an excuse in the court of law. An ignorant child of God will be harassed or taken advantage off by Satan plus his agents and such a person may not receive or experience all of God's promises.

How to overcome ignorance:

- ◈ Identify the areas of your ignorance e.g. is it academic, financial, spiritual, emotional?
- ◈ Identify the reason for your ignorance.
- ◈ Acknowledge the ignorance.
- ◈ Confess your ignorance to God.
- ◈ Take positive steps to overcome the ignorance by searching for the necessary information from the right persons or quarters.
- ◈ Enlarge your reading horizon.
- ◈ Stop pretending you know when you don't.
- ◈ Ask for help where and when possible. If someone turns you down, approach another person but test all spirits and hold on to that which is true (*1 John 4:1*).
- ◈ There is help and hope for you. You just need to seek, search and ask.

Exercise:

- In what ways have you been ignorant before?
- Why were you ignorant?
- What did your ignorance cost you or your family or community?
- What steps did you take or have you taken to overcome your ignorance?
- If you have overcome your ignorance, share your testimony. It will help others who might be struggling in that very thing; it will bring Glory to God and shame to the devil.

Prayer Points:

Lord, I confess all of my ignorance to You and ask for mercy and forgiveness in Jesus name.

Father, please help me not be ignorant in matters of life.

Lord, in Your name and with Your help please deliver me from every form of ignorance.

'Let's Reason Together ...Youths' A-Z

MY PERSONAL NOTES

JEALOUSY

"Jealousy opens me up to lack of peace."

"... jealousy is as hard {and} cruel as Sheol (the place of the dead). Its flashes are flashes of fire, a most vehement flame [the very flame of the Lord]!" [Song of Solomon 8:6].

Questions For Consideration/Discussion:
1. What is jealousy?
2. What makes people jealous?
3. Is jealousy a sin or not and why?
4. Can jealousy be used positively?

What is Jealousy?

Jealousy can be described as an attitude of envy, covetousness, resentment or protectiveness. It is a dangerous and wicked spirit that comes as a result of comparing one's self with others. Shakespeare called jealousy the green-eyed monster. An unchecked jealous attitude may make a person want to take what belongs to others or destroy what makes others happy.

What makes people jealous?

Jealousy comes secondary to the lack of contentment with whom or what they have or what they have achieved.

Is jealousy a sin or not and why?

Jealousy that makes one do the wrong things in order to satisfy it or that ends up destroying others is a sin. Joseph's brothers sold him into slavery because of their jealousy. Yet at God's own time he was appointed to become the first Prime Minister in Egypt. What his half brothers meant for evil God turned into good *(Genesis 37- 45)*. Cain killed Abel out of jealousy, God saw it all and he was severely punished and banished from God. *Genesis 4:1-18.*

JEALOUSY

After David killed Goliath, the women sang a song saying *"Saul has killed his thousands, and David his ten thousands!"* Instead of King Saul to thank the Lord, he became unnecessarily jealous of David and sought for ways to kill him *(1 Samuel 18: 6-26; 1 Samuel 19:9-17)*. Because of this, God took His anointing of peace from Saul and he was oppressed by a tormenting spirit. Being jealous of others will open you up to satanic oppression of many forms.

Can jealousy be used positively or can anything good come out of jealousy?

Just like jealousy can lead a person to do the wrong things, jealousy when properly channelled can make a person do some things better, e.g. reading and studying the Bible more so that I can quote as many verses as Brother A or Sister B when witnessing or praying; or taking my studies more seriously so that I can be in the top five in my class.

EXERCISE:

- In what ways have you been jealous before and why?
- What was the consequence of your jealousy on yourself and others?
- Have you ever experienced anything like positive jealousy?
- Is there anyone that you are jealous of? Why?
- How can you bring something good out of your jealousy?

PRAYER POINTS:

Lord, please forgive me for all the times I have been unnecessarily jealous of others.

Father, please help me from now never to be jealous of anyone else.

Lord, please bless me and get me to Your designed position and place for my life irrespective of the so many acts of jealousy around and against me.

JEALOUSY

MY PERSONAL NOTES

KINDNESS

"Kindness is being good to your fellow men."

"For His mercy {and} loving-kindness are great toward us, and the truth {and} faithfulness of the Lord endure forever. Praise the Lord! (Hallelujah!)."

[Psalm 117:2]

Questions For Consideration/ Discussion:
1. What is kindness?
2. Why do we need to be kind?
3. To whom do I need to be kind?
4. Rewards of showing kindness.

What is kindness?

This is an attitude or action that shows thoughtfulness towards another person or thing. It shows compassion, humanity, sympathy, consideration, gentleness, helpfulness and benevolence.

Why do we need to be kind?

It is good to be good and it is nice to be kind. To reap kindness you and I need to sow kindness as often and as practicable as we can.

To whom do I need to be kind?

To as many people that you meet in life in need of kindness, love and mercy especially those whom you know cannot pay you back i.e. the less fortunate, dejected, rejected and poor in your community, the unloving, unlovely and unlovable. Jonathan showed kindness to David who was not in a position to pay back but many years later David showed kindness unto Jonathan's son. Mephibosheth, *(2Samuel 9:1-13)*. Only the Samaritan showed kindness to the man who had been robbed, beaten and wounded on the way to Jericho *(Luke 10:30- 37)*. Be aware that God notices and records your every act of kindness. Equally important to know is that not all acts of kindness brings a reward; at times it may bring pain or even death on earth but always commendation from God.

We need to show kindness to other creatures of God e.g. animals, birds, fish etc.

Rewards of showing kindness

These include:
- Self satisfaction,
- God's joyful approval,
- God's blessings,
- Love and appreciation of people,
- Blessings from the people we have been kind to,
- Blessings in folds to your children and seed.

EXERCISE:

- ❖ In what ways have you shown or received kindness of late?
- ❖ Why did you show kindness at that time?
- ❖ What did showing kindness do to you?
- ❖ Will you continue to show kindness? Why or why not?

PRAYER POINTS:

Lord, thank You for putting in me Your seed of kindness.

Father, please grant unto me the grace of extending Your type of kindness to all that I meet with from now on in Jesus name.

Lord, please help me that I might be kind and trustworthy from now in Jesus name.

'Let's Reason Together ...Youths' A-Z

MY PERSONAL NOTES

LAWFUL

"Lawful does not mean helpful or useful."

"Everything is permissible (allowable and lawful) for me; but not all things are helpful (good for me to do, expedient and profitable when considered with other things). Everything is lawful for me, but I will not become the slave of anything {or} be brought under its power."
[1 Corinthians 6:12].

Questions For Consideration/ Discussion:
1. What does it mean for something to be lawful?
2. Why do we have laws?
3. Examples of lawful acts or habits.
4. Is everything lawfully good for you or not?
5. How do I differentiate 'good' from lawful?
6. Can you become a slave of a lawful thing?

What does it mean for something to be lawful?

It means that something is legal, legally recognized, official, officially recognized, legitimate, endorsed or allowed. There are at least two types of laws operating in the world today – God's laws as contained in the Bible and – man's law as contained in the country or state's constitution. Before anyone can say something is legal it must be with reference to one of these two laws. God's law has outlived all man made laws and from it people have coined their laws for their own purpose. God's law primarily governs Christians and it is most comprehensive and fairer than any man made law. God's laws are written in the Bible to guide, guard and protect us. They are not written to limit us or curtail our joy, as our God is not a joy killer.

Why do we have laws?

Laws are made to protect lives, safeguard properties, ensure and promote peace and justice, demarcate boundaries as to what is acceptable and not acceptable by the lawmaker.

LAWFUL

Some examples of lawful acts or habits

Kindness, working, studying, marriage, having a family, helping others etc.

Is everything lawful good for you or not?

The fact that something is lawful does not necessarily make it good or beneficial to a person. Although drinking alcohol and smoking are permitted after age 16 in some countries e.g. UK, and prostitution and abortion might be lawful, they are not good for anybody. All these can kill or destroy the person doing them or other people around him or her.

For example it is a known fact that smoking cuts down the life of the smoker and negatively affects the lives of those who inhale the smoke; it leads to so many terrible diseases and thousands in the UK die daily from smoking related diseases. Many also have to shop lift, steal, kill or sell their bodies in order to get money for their smoking habits. Some, who graduated from smoking cigarette into cannabis etc, have ended in mental institutions, sometimes permanently destroyed.

Unmarried people who indulge in premarital sex do not only expose themselves to various forms of sexually transmitted diseases, curable and incurable but also to unplanned and unwanted pregnancy, heartache, bitterness, anger, frustration, lack of trust, etc. To cover up unwanted pregnancy some end up having abortions, which is killing the unborn baby – though permitted by law in some communities, it is against God's laws as contained in the Bible. For some unfortunate ladies, this has led to their own serious handicap or physical death due to complications, guilt or inability to conceive later in life when they now feel settled and ready for a family. In many cases, the man responsible for the aborted pregnancy abandons the lady and she may suffer from guilt and at times, nightmares.

Kindness, working, studying, marriage, having a family, helping others are all lawful and good for anybody. These acts help the person and others.

How do I differentiate 'good' from lawful?

The society in which we live today keeps changing goal posts with regards to what is good or not but to be safe at all times, check with the Bible. God does not change and neither do His words or principles. His laws are to make us live to the fullest in peace and enjoyment. Once you use the Bible as your guide on any issue, you can never go wrong.

LAWFUL

It was lawful for Daniel and his friends to eat from the king's meal but they chose another menu of vegetables and water, which they considered better not only for their health, memory, sound judgement etc. but because the food offered by the king had been sacrificed to the king's idol which was against their belief in Yaweh *(Daniel 1: 1- 20)*.

While it is lawful to eat fatty foods it is not good for the body. Obesity is a cause of many diseases in both the young and old. In the Old Testament, all animal fat in the sacrifice offered to God was to be burned in fire not eaten; but today we find it in many foods. Too much sugar in food or drink could lead to hyperactivity and tooth decay amongst other things. Whilst the Bible does not have say do not eat too much sugar, it certainly says our body is the temple of God: that being the case, we must carefully consider what we eat, wear, and do to our bodies.

Can you become a slave of a lawful thing?

Anyone who does not exercise good self-control can become a slave of a lawful thing. For example, it is lawful to eat but if that is not controlled, the person may end up living only for food. The results of overeating includes becoming gluttonous, obesity and its aftermaths, inability to spend quality time on other profitable ventures. A believer ought only to be slaves of God not of any man or thing however good.

LAWFUL

Exercise:

- List examples of lawful and unlawful things or acts.
- From your list, identify those that are good for you, those that are bad and why.
- Identify someone in the Bible who did or did not perform lawful acts.
- What can we learn from this person?
- What lawful thing have you become a slave to and why?
- Describe how you prayerfully plan to overcome this habit.

Prayer Points:

Lord, please help me to differentiate between lawful, helpful and useful.

Father, I refuse the manifestations of all unlawful laws in my life, destiny, family and community in Jesus name.

Lord, please help me not to succumb to pressures that are ungodly, unlawful or un helpful.

MONEY

*"My worth is not in the money
I have or don't have."*

*"For the love of money is the root of all evils."
[1 Timothy 6:10a].*

Questions For Consideration/Discussion
1. What is money?
2. Why do we need money?
3. Is it evil or sinful to have money?
4. Rewards of having money.
5. Money and the gospel.

What is money?

Money is defined as riches, capital, investment, funds, wealth, currency cash or change. It is one of the means of trading or of assessing the value of a product or service. Money is one of the mediums of financial transaction. Every community has its own money also known as currency e.g. in Nigeria the currency is naira and kobo, in the UK, it is pounds and pence; in USA it is dollars and cents.

Why do we need money?

We need money for transacting business, for payment of goods and services, for assessing the value/worth of a product or service.

How can I have money?

Some are born into wealth, which they inherit but most people have to work and earn an income before they have money. Unless the money inherited is unlimited, the beneficiary may not have to work but most wise people with inheritance still go and work, looking for ways of having more income. Working is scriptural for the Bible says anyone (who is fit to but who refuses to) work should not

MONEY

eat. Importantly, the work done should be what is lawful, not contradictory to the laws of God. Prostitution, stealing, robbery, killing etc. may be some kind of work but they do not glorify God and so should not be done by a Christian.

To have money:
- Be willing to work for the money for what you do not work for, you will hardly value.
- Pay your tithes as commanded by God i.e. 10% of all your earnings and gifts *(Genesis 14:17-20; Malachi 3:10-12,)*
- Give freewill offerings i.e. this is not specified but according to your appreciation of God's goodness unto you.
- Have a financial plan for yourself and use it over and over again.
- Consider ways such as investments in which you can make your money work for you not vice-versa.
- Give generously to the work of God, the Church, and the less privileged.
- Expect a miracle from the Lord.

Is it evil or sinful to have money?

It is not evil to have money or be wealthy. It is evil for money to have you. God our Father is exceedingly rich such that the streets of heaven where He lives and where one day the believer is going to be living with Him are paved with gold. However, it is very evil to love money or acquire it fraudulently. Money is to be used not worshipped. It is equally evil to be selfish with our money not sharing it, or giving to the Lord. We should be careful not to make money our god for it has wings like the bird *(Proverbs 23:5)*.

Rewards of having money

Money, the Bible says answers all things. Money can be used to bless and serve mankind. It can be used to purchase technology that will make any work easier and goals to be achieved quicker. Money can be used to spread the gospel.

Money and the gospel are they related?

Sharing the gospel i.e. the good news of Jesus Christ requires money. There is a popular phrase that money is the wheel on which the gospel rides. Whilst the message of Jesus Christ is the same forever, the method of spreading the good news keeps changing in order to reach all men. For example some people prefer listening to the Bible on tapes/CD or watching it on DVD's or video tapes rather than sitting down to read the printed copy. Some have the e-version on their palm or lap tops or iPad, which may be easier for them to read and carry around.

Your monetary blessings should be reflected in your giving unto various Christian avenues of spreading the gospel and helping the needy.

EXERCISE:

- ◈ How will you rate your love of money / earthly goods?
- ◈ What are you prepared to do to get more money than you have now?
- ◈ Have you been struggling with having to pay your tithes and offering? If so why?
- ◈ Evaluate how much of your money you have sown into the spreading of the gospel.
- ◈ Is money working for you or are you working for money?
- ◈ Is money your slave or you are a slave of money?
- ◈ Money answers all things. How?

PRAYER POINTS:

Lord, please help me so that my love for You will always be greater than the love for any material wealth.

Father, please enrich me for Your Glory and the blessings of mankind.

Lord, please teach my hands to make good profit in my endeavours in life and may money begin to work for me as from now in Jesus name.

MONEY

NAME

"A good name is far better than riches."

"Therefore [because He stooped so low] God has highly exalted Him and has freely bestowed on Him the name that is above every name, That in (at) the name of Jesus every knee should (must) bow, in heaven and on earth and under the earth, And every tongue [frankly and openly] confess {and} acknowledge that Jesus Christ is Lord, to the glory of God the Father."
[Philippians 2: 9 -11]

Questions for Consideration/Discussion
1. What is a name?
2. What is your name and what does your name mean?
3. What is a good name?
4. What is the name of the Lord?

What is a name?

A name is the unique identification given to a thing or person to differentiate it from others. After God finished with His work of creation, He brought all the beasts of the field and the fowls of the air to Adam to name *(Genesis 2:19-20)*. Human beings also give names to their children. Some parents name their children after a person, a thing that means much to them, or circumstances that have impacted their life e.g. some name their children Chelsea after the football club, others after a river, celebrity, place or event. In some cultures, giving a child a name is so significant that it might take a few days or weeks after the child's birth for the parents or heads of their clan to come up with a suitable one.

What is your name and what does it mean?

Should you find that your name does not glorify God or is causing you trouble like the case of Jabez (1 Chronicles 4:9-10) or Nabal (1 Samuel 25:1-25), take it to the Lord in prayer and seek godly counsel if necessary.

NAME

What is a good name?

A good name is one that brings along with it good memories, joy, excitement, positive aura. Whatever good you invest in other people's lives will outlive you and bring glory to God. Such was the name of Dorcas *(Acts 9:36-42)*. It is not uncommon for people to change their names these days if it has a negative impact on their lives. God changed some names in the Bible e.g. Abram was changed to Abraham, Sarai to Sarah, Jacob the trickster to Israel, the prince of God.

Does your name or nickname, give glory to God or is it associated with any form of evil? Do you need a new name? If yes, you probably need a touch of the Holy Spirit and you may equally need a character change.

The name of the Lord

The names of the Lord are innumerable, as they tend to describe the attributes of God. The Lord often chooses to reveal just a finite part of Himself to mankind; we then describe Him in the light of that revelation. God's names describe Him as best as possible in our own understanding. He created all and was not created. He is referred to as the

Ancient of days, without an end; the beginning and end of all things, the Alpha and the Omega. His name is above all other names known or unknown, in every generation.

It is through the name of the Lord that our protection, provision and direction are secured (Proverbs 18:10).

NAME

Exercise:

◈ Everyone in the group should mention their names and tell others the meaning of their names.
◈ If you are using this book by yourself, list all your names and find out their meanings from your parents or older siblings.
◈ What is your nickname/street name if you have one?
◈ What does that nickname/street name mean?
◈ Is there any of your names that you would rather change and why?
◈ Mention at least seven names of God that are special to you and say why.

Prayer Points:

Lord, forgive me for all the bad names I have been given or acquired.

Father, in Your mercy please give me a new name that will reflect Your destiny for my life ahead not of my past.

Lord, please help me to consciously remember that I bear Your name and so live a life that will always honour You.

NAME

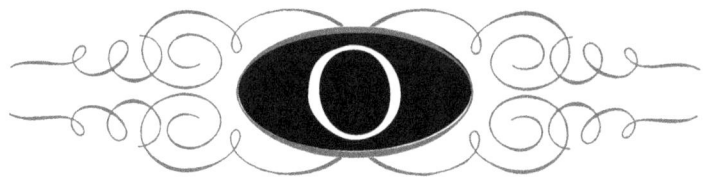

OBEDIENCE

"It pays to be obedient."

"Behold, to obey is better than sacrifice, and to hearken than the fat of rams."
[1 Samuel 15:22b].

Questions for Consideration/ Discussion:
1. What is obedience?
2. Who we need to obey
3. Why the need for obedience?
4. Are young people obedient today?
5. When and where is obedience required?
6. Results of obedience.
7. Should you obey when you are being abused?
8. Should you obey when the authority is walking contrary to the Bible?

What is obedience?

Obedience means many things including submission, agreement to, conformity, compliance, deference, and concurrence. It may also be used in relationship with duty that is performed.

Who do we need to obey?

We are to obey God and those He has put in charge to look after our well being – our parents, older siblings, elderly people in our extended family including aunties and uncles; as well as teachers both at school and in the Church. In addition we have the law of the land that governs the welfare of the society in which we live. There is also the word of God, which when obeyed gives a successful and rewarding life.

Why the need for obedience?

Obedience is necessary for our protection, guidance and provision. Whilst it may be true that many young people have knowledge, which their parents don't possess, it is equally true that they lack the experience of adults. Experience comes with age and it will protect more than academic knowledge can. Experience can predict the end of a matter at its beginning, which knowledge may not be able to do. A popular Nigerian adage says when the youth is cutting a tree in the forest; the on looking adult already knows where it will fall.

The laws of the land in which you live ought to be obeyed for they were set up for the welfare, protection and smooth running of a civilised society in which you reside. Most importantly, the Bible is to be obeyed. It contains God's love letter to mankind, it gives guidance, hope, encouragement, correction, direction and warnings. If obeyed, you will have a successful life here on earth and it will give you a place in heaven.

Are young people obedient today?

Young people may find it more difficult to be obedient today because of many reasons including any or all of the following:
- thinking they are smarter than their parents, elders, teachers or pastors.
- thinking they are being unnecessarily curtailed, monitored or teleguided.
- need for autonomy.
- rebellious spirit.

- ❖ where the authority e.g. parents are walking contrary to what they are telling them to do.
- ❖ where there is no parental guidance.
- ❖ where the authority in question has abused or is abusing the young person.
- ❖ negative peer pressure.
- ❖ wrong information.
- ❖ where the authority in question lacks credible integrity.

When and where is obedience required?

Obedience is necessary at all times and everywhere. It is not unusual that the school, church, home, and general community has written and unwritten rules which everyone; youth inclusive is expected to live by. The school expects pupils not to play truancy or fight or cheat during examinations. In the home, there ought to be love, as well as acceptance. In the community, obeying all traffic rules and so on is important.

Results of obedience

Obedience has many positive effects. For example, it will get you out of trouble most times but should it land you in trouble like Joseph, be assured that God will rescue you.

OBEDIENCE

Obedience gives protection and brings peace and prosperity. Persistent disobedience is called rebellion, which can be likened to witchcraft or black magic.

Should you obey when you are being abused?

Once this has been identified, the young person should immediately seek godly counsel before the situation gets more complicated. As every case is unique, it is difficult to prescribe a universal approach to this situation. Young people being abused should prayerfully seek for help from those who would believe them and if need be, get out of the location of abuse without delay.
(Please refer to pages 217 –218)

Should you obey when the authority is walking contrary to the Bible?

For as long as your obedience is in line with the Bible, that of what the authority is doing should not deter you from doing what is right.

** Group coordinator should please provide confidential sex counselling and prayers and seek for help if and where needed at the end of it.

EXERCISE:

- ◈ Who are you supposed to obey?
- ◈ Why do you have to obey anyone else?
- ◈ Why do you have to obey God?
- ◈ In what ways can you demonstrate your obedience?
- ◈ Give examples of times when it was difficult for you to obey.
- ◈ List some rewards of obedience that you have enjoyed.

PRAYER POINTS:

Lord, please forgive me for all my partial obedience and total disobedience to You and the authorities over me.

Father, please grant me a heart that is obedient to You always as from now so that I might eat of the good of the land. Isaiah 1:18-20.

Lord, please grant unto me the grace to obey all the authorities over me in line with Your words from now on.

'Let's Reason Together ...Youths' A-Z

MY PERSONAL NOTES

PRAISE

"I am alive therefore I will praise the Lord."

"I will bless the Lord at all times; His praise shall continually be in my mouth."
[Psalm 34:1]

Questions For Consideration/Discussion
1. What is praise?
2. Who do we need to praise?
3. How do I praise God?
4. When do we need to praise God?
5. How do we praise others?
6. What is the difference between praising God and praising a person?
7. Can we always praise God?
8. What happens when we do not praise God?

What is praise?

Praise may mean many things including going into raptures over, exalting, commending, eulogizing, admiring or worshipping a being, person or thing. It may also mean congratulating or paying tribute or applauding or acclaiming a being or person. Praise is usually done openly i.e. by our action e.g. writing, talking, singing and dancing. Praise has also been defined as an acronym for:

P- Powerful
R- Resistance
A- Against the
I- Intimidation and
S- Strategy of the
E- Enemy

Who do we need to praise?

We need to praise God our creator and Sustainer for He alone is worthy of our adoration and praise; when praises go up, blessings come down. If we refuse to praise God, Jesus said God is able to raise stones to praise Him in our place *(Luke 19:37-40)*. God also ordained praise because it is a powerful tool for overcoming the enemy as we see in the story of Jehoshaphat and his people *(2 Chronicles 20:15-25)*. If all fails try praise!

PRAISE

How do we praise God?

Praising God could be done through our verbal expressions e.g. in songs, talking to Him in prayer, sharing with others, dancing unto the Lord etc. It could also be done through various acts of gratitude e.g. giving to people in need, trying to help others in whatever ways possible to show our gratitude to God.

When do we need to praise God?

At all times and in all situations just as it says in *Psalms 34:1*. Praise God in times of peace and in times of war, in times of health and in times of ill health, in times of plenty and in times of lack, in times of certainty and in times of uncertainty, in times of success and in times of failure, in times of life and in times of death, in season and out of season, in times of storms and in times of calm, we must praise God. He is able and willing to rescue us in times of trouble. He can change our situation around positively in the twinkling of an eye. He also makes all things work together for the good of those who love Him and are called according to His purpose *(Romans 8:28)*.

How do we praise others?

We praise others as we thank them, congratulate them, applaud their achievement or help but we are never to worship them for they are human beings like us.

What is the difference between praising God and praising a person?

Praising God usually leads us into a time of worship of God. Praising any person should not lead to us worshipping them for God alone deserves our worship.

Can we always praise God?

Difficult as it may be, we, like Job, can still praise God in all situations *(Job 13:15)*. We may not understand what and why what happened but believing fully well that God is in control and able to save us in every situation, we can praise Him.

PRAISE

What happens when we do not praise God?

Deliberate refusal to praise God opens one up to the devil. It is an act of in-gratitude and if care is not taken, a person may begin to loose what he/she has taken for granted.

PRAISE

EXERCISE:

❖ What does praising God mean to you?
❖ Share with others occasions when you have praised God and what for.
❖ Was there any time you found it hard to praise God? If yes, why?
❖ How do you usually praise God?
❖ Why should a person praise God?

PRAYER POINTS:

Lord, I am very grateful for the privilege of praising You.

Father, please teach and help me to praise You in every situation that I find myself. Psalms 34:1-end.

Lord, may Your praise never cease from my mouth. heart, life and family from now on in Jesus name.

MY PERSONAL NOTES

'Let's Reason Together ...Youths' A-Z

QUIET TIME

"Prayer is the master key to every situation in life."

"For thus said the Lord God, the Holy One of Israel: In returning [to Me] and resting [in Me] you shall be saved; in quietness and in [trusting] confidence shall be your strength. But you would not," [Isaiah 30:15].

Questions for Consideration/ Discussion:
1. What is quiet time?
2. Why do you need quiet time and with whom?
3. When do we need quiet time?
4. How often do you need quiet time?
5. Where should I have my quiet time?
6. What do you do in your quiet time?
7. Rewards of having quiet time.
8. What keeps you from having quiet times?

What is quiet time?

As the name suggests it is time spent in the presence of the Lord ministering to and receiving from Him.

Why do you need quiet time and with whom?

Mankind was made to rule over all other creation and to fellowship with God. A properly used quiet time affords us the opportunity of being in the presence of the Lord. Just as being part of a family involves getting to know the members of the family as much as it is possible, having quiet time with the Lord gives us the opportunity of getting to know Him better by speaking to and hearing from Him, as well as receiving love, counsel and blessings from Him. Every child of God ought to have regular quiet time with Him.

When do you need quiet time?

In good and bad times, in pleasant and unpleasant times, in plenty and in scarcity – in all situations, we need quiet time.

QUIET TIME

How often do you need quiet time?

God is everywhere and ever ready to spend some time with us. As such, we ought to seek Him as often as practicable all through the day.

Where should I have my quiet time?

Much as God is everywhere, we can pray everywhere and anywhere not necessarily disturbing others or not performing our expected duties. In praying, learning to turn our thoughts and confessions into prayers is one of the ways of praying round the clock without ceasing. Since we do not need to shut our eyes before having a thought or being able to talk/speak we can pray any and everywhere. As we drive to work, do our housework; write our reports we can pray, in order words in whatever we are doing we can still be praying. However it is nice for each one to find a place and time that best suits the person as the primary place of having the quiet time. When I was growing up, privacy for anything was very challenging so I decided to always have my quiet time in the loo *(toilet, restroom)* as no one was going to disturb me there and I kept it very clean. Some of the best revelations had been given to me whilst sitting on the toilet seat and having my quite time!

What do we do in our quiet time?

We must use our quiet time wisely and profitably. Some people spend their quiet time reading the Bible and hearing God speak to them; some worship and praise Him, others meditate on the scriptures or on an attribute or more of God e.g. love, holiness etc. For others, quiet time is used for praying and writing specific instructions from God.

Rewards of having quiet time

Being in the presence of God has many benefits including:
- Reflecting His glory e.g. Moses *(Exodus 34:29-35)*
- Wisdom in making choices.
- Supernatural gift of healing.
- Ability to teach with wisdom.
- Divine ideas and revelations.
- Ability to recognise God's leading/leadership.
- Entering into God's rest for comfort and strength.

What keeps us from having quiet times?

This could be due to any one or a combination of the following:
- Taking God for granted.

QUIET TIME

- Ingratitude to God.
- Poor management of our time – someone has said time is an equal opportunity employer giving all people irrespective of their gender, culture, age, weakness or strength etc. the same 24 hours to trade with daily.
- Distractions from within and / or outside which could be self set up or devil imposed.
- Bad company/wrong influence/negative peer pressure.
- Guilt and fear from sin.
- Rebellion against God.
- Unanswered prayers in the past.

EXERCISE:

- ❖ On a scale of 10, with 10 being your having the best time with God in fellowship, how would you rate your quiet time now?
- ❖ Where can you have your quiet time?
- ❖ Why do you need to have quiet time?
- ❖ What do you do in your quiet time?
- ❖ When is the best time for you to have quiet time?
- ❖ How does God speak to you in your quiet time?
- ❖ How does your quiet time affect your spiritual walk with God?
- ❖ Is anything or anyone keeping you away from having quiet times these days? If there is, then please identify who or what it is and seek for mature counselling and prayers.

PRAYER POINTS:

Lord, thank You that I can come to You just as I am anytime, anywhere and for any reason.

Father, please forgive me for not keeping the quiet time appointments with You often.

Lord, I need Thee every moment of life, please help me to stay in Your presence in the place of praise, prayers and meditation of Your words.

Prayerfully meditate on this song by Annie S. Hawks, 1872.
Music: Robert Lowry (MIDI, NWC, PDF).

I need Thee every hour, most gracious Lord;
No tender voice like Thine can peace afford.
Refrain
I need Thee, O I need Thee;
Every hour I need Thee;
O bless me now, my Savior,
I come to Thee.

I need Thee every hour, stay Thou nearby;
Temptations lose their power when Thou art nigh.
Refrain

I need Thee every hour, in joy or pain;
Come quickly and abide, or life is in vain.
Refrain

I need Thee every hour; teach me Thy will;
And Thy rich promises in me fulfill.
Refrain

I need Thee every hour, most Holy One;
O make me Thine indeed, Thou blessèd Son.
Refrain

Source : http://www.hymntime.com/tch/htm/i/n/ineedteh.htm

QUIET TIME

REJECTION

"I am special to God and He will never reject me."

"Jesus asked them, Have you never read in the Scriptures: The very Stone which the builders rejected {and} threw away has become the Cornerstone; this is the Lord's doing, and it is marvelous in our eyes?" [Matthew 21:42].

Questions for Consideration/Discussion
1. What is rejection?
2. What causes rejection?
3. Symptoms of rejection.
4. Results/effects of rejection.
5. How to deal with rejection.
6. Can God reject anyone?

What is Rejection?

It is a negative response to someone or something, a refusal or denial of rights and entitlements, a rebuff, refutation or denunciation, dismissal or elimination. Rejection is mostly painful to the one who has been rejected.

What causes rejection?

Rejection could be due to what is humanly perceived as the selection of the best or fittest among many possible others for the same position or opportunity. It may also be secondary to discrimination or feeling of threat by the person who has rejected you, e.g. in some job interviews. One could be rejected for what you have or don't have, what you do or don't do, where you come or don't come from, whose child you are or not are, some are even rejected on the basis of what they have to offer in a relationship, or for their looks, education, vocation or handicap. Human rejection for a believer could be God ordained in order for His will to come to pass in the person's life.

Symptoms of Rejection:

◈ This can show up in several ways including:

- Withdrawal from others under any flimsy excuse.
- Change of mood or character.
- Excessive quietness much more than usual for that person.
- Weeping.
- Sickness.

Results / effects of rejection

Rejection is a common life experience. What matters is how each person reacts when it comes. Rejection can be either a building stone to a higher position or a reason to wallow in self-pity and go much further down. When God rejected the offering of Cain he became angry and later killed Abel *(Genesis 4:1-8)*. Joseph's rejection by his half brothers led him to slavery in Egypt and, his own rejection of Portiphar's wife landed him in the prison where he later met his destiny helper *(Genesis 39 – 41)*.

How to deal with rejection:

- Acknowledge the rejection but focus on God.
- Don't believe the lie of the devil that you are not good or beautiful enough etc.

- Try to find out why you were rejected and what or how you can learn from it.
- Refuse to give in to self-pity or thinking and speaking negatively.
- Remember that God loves you irrespective of man's opinion of you.
- Don't believe any person's report that contradicts God's report of you.
- Trust God to use your rejection to honour, bless and promote you.

Permit me to share with you this write up titled, **"12 Healthy Attitudes towards Myself"** from The Word for Today:

1. I know God created me and that He loves me – *Jeremiah 31:3.*
2. I have shortcomings and I want to change. I believe that God is working in my life each day; while He is, I can still accept and enjoy myself.
3. Everyone has faults; I am not a failure because I am not perfect.
4. I am working with God to overcome my faults, but there will always be something to work on; therefore I will not be discouraged when He convicts me on areas that need improvement.

5. I want people to like me but my sense of worth is not dependent on them. Jesus has already demonstrated my worth by dying for me.
6. I will not be controlled by what others say, think or do. If they reject me I will survive, for God has promised never to reject me as long as I keep on believing.
7. No matter how often I fail I will not give up, because God is with me, He has promised to strengthen and to sustain me as long as I live. *Hebrews 13:5.*
8. I like myself, I do not like everything I do, and I want to change- but I refuse to put myself down.
9. I am acceptable to God through the blood of Jesus. *Ephesians 2:8-9.*
10. God has a plan for my life and I am going to fulfil it; I have God- given gifts and I intend to use them to glorify Him.
11. I, by myself, am nothing, but in Christ I am everything I need to be.
12. I can do whatever God calls me to do, through the power of Him who dwells in me. *Philippians 4:14.* Amen.

© WORD FOR TODAY 2000

Can God reject anyone?

God hates sin but rejects no one, not even a murderer. There is room in the heart of God for anyone who believes that through Christ Jesus, there is forgiveness for every prodigal 'child' who will return home.

Have you experienced rejection or do you know someone who has? You might want to prayerfully meditate on this song written by Philip P. Bliss in 1870:

> *I am so glad that our Father in Heav'n*
> *Tells of His love in the Book He has giv'n;*
> *Wonderful things in the Bible I see,*
> *This is the dearest, that Jesus loves me.*
> *Refrain*
> *I am so glad that Jesus loves me,*
> *Jesus loves me, Jesus loves me.*
> *I am so glad that Jesus loves me,*
> *Jesus loves even me.*
>
> *Though I forget Him, and wander away,*
> *Still He doth love me wherever I stray;*
> *Back to His dear loving arms I do flee,*
> *When I remember that Jesus loves me.*
> *Refrain*
>
> *Oh, if there's only one song I can sing,*
> *When in His beauty I see the great King,*
> *This shall my song through eternity be,*
> *"Oh, what a wonder that Jesus loves me!"*

Refrain

Jesus loves me, and I know I love Him;
Love brought Him down my poor soul to redeem;
Yes, it was love made Him die on the tree;
Oh, I am certain that Jesus loves me!
Refrain

If one should ask of me, how can I tell?
Glory to Jesus, I know very well!
God's Holy Spirit with mine doth agree,
Constantly witnessing Jesus loves me.
Refrain

In this assurance I find sweetest rest,
Trusting in Jesus, I know I am blessed;
Satan, dismayed, from my soul now doth flee,
When I just tell him that Jesus loves me.
Refrain

Source- Words and music on http://www.cyberhymnal.org/htm/
j/l/jlovesem.htm

EXERCISE:

◈ In what ways have you experienced rejection?
◈ What has rejection cost you personally?
◈ How have coped or are you coping with rejection?
◈ Are there things that you can do to reduce your chances of being rejected in future? i.e. self-improvement measures such as go to school, learn a trade, study more, dress and act better etc.
◈ In what ways have you rejected another person and why?

PRAYER POINTS:

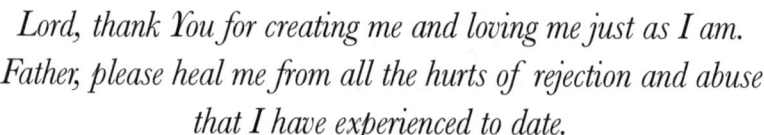

Lord, thank You for creating me and loving me just as I am. Father, please heal me from all the hurts of rejection and abuse that I have experienced to date.

Father, please forgive me for rejecting the following people (mention their names) and help me to love them as You do from now on.

Lord, please constantly remind me that my self worth is only in You not in myself, what I have or don't have, do or don't do.

REJECTION

SEX

"With God's help I will keep my marriage bed undefiled."

"Let marriage be held in honor (esteemed worthy, precious, of great price, and especially dear) in all things. And thus let the marriage bed be undefiled (kept undishonored); for God will judge {and} punish the unchaste [all guilty of sexual vice] and adulterous." [Hebrews 13:4]

Questions For Consideration/ Discussion:
1. What is sex?
2. Whose idea was sex?
3. Is there truly anything like "safe sex"?
4. "No sex." Is that possible at my age?
5. With whom should I have sex?
6. How do I deal with or satisfy my sexual hunger?
7. Sex and love are they the same?

8. Once defiled, can I be made whole again?
9. Is it sinful or harmful to remain a virgin until my marriage?
10. Can I still be a virgin whilst practising oral or anal sex?
11. Is masturbating safe or is it sinful?
12. How to deal with sexual abuse.

SEX

What is sex?

For the purpose of this discussion, the word sex is used to mean intercourse between two people of opposite gender.

Whose idea was sex?

God ordained sex between a man and woman married to one another *(Genesis 1:28; 2)*. Adam had all the animals with him in the garden before Eve was created yet he did not make any move to have a relationship or intercourse with any of them. God ordained sex between a married couple i.e. man and woman not between same gender or humans and any beast tamed or untamed. Such is simply an abomination to God *(Leviticus 18:1-end)*. Animals make love to the opposite gender of their kind i.e. male lion with a female lion not anther male lion; and not male or female lion with a tiger or monkey, so there is no natural justification for same sex marriage or sexual intercourse between a human being and any animal. You will also not see animals having anal sex yet God has made mankind to be wiser than animals.

Is there truly anything like "safe sex"?

Two things are commonly considered with the phrase

"safe sex" i.e. having sexual intercourse without the fear of resulting pregnancy and equally, if not more importantly, the idea of not transmitting or being infected with sexually transmitted diseases like gonorrhoea, herpes, syphilis, HIV/AIDS etc. Both reasons have significant consequences that can last a person's lifetime therefore the universal campaign for "safe sex". However, the only truly safe sex is no sex at all until after your marriage, while for the married couple, safe sex means keeping to your husband or wife only as long as you both live i.e. no adultery. Using condoms or any other contraceptive device outside of marriage is not God's idea. Moreover, condoms do sometimes tear whilst in use and according to manufacturers themselves, no medical device is 100% safe.

Spiritually, because sexual intercourse involves an exchange of body fluid, the act becomes more of a covenant than just a casual affair. Each time you have sexual intercourse you leave part of yourself with that person and take a part of him or her also. in the process, some have unknowingly inherited curses, yokes, diseases, etc. from their sleeping partners.

"No sex." Is that possible at my age?

God ordained sexual intercourse within the context of

marriage only. It is possible with God's help not to have sexual intercourse at any age.

With whom should I have sex?

Sexual intercourse should only be with your spouse. Rather than sleeping around or burning with lust, the Bible says such a person should get married *(1 Corinthians 7:1-2)*.

How do I deal with or satisfy my sexual hunger?

It is not uncommon for teenagers or young adults to experience some sexual urges due to hormonal changes but the Bible says if you cannot wait due to pressures from within and without, then get married as only sexual intercourse within this context is permissible. Nevertheless, there is more to marriage than sex. Marriage is for the prepared, unselfish, whole person. If you are struggling with controlling your sexual inclinations, then I suggest you do the following:
- ❖ Accept that you have a challenge in this area.
- ❖ Come clean before the Lord confessing your sin and lack of self control in this area of your life.
- ❖ Ask the Lord to show you what you need to do to get over this challenge.

- ◆ Watch what you feed your mind & spirit, avoid pornographic materials – video, television, literature and audios that will continue to defile your mind and spirit.
- ◆ Avoid bad company.
- ◆ Spend more time reading Godly materials and meditating on scriptures for the washing of your spirit and renewing of your mind.
- ◆ Avoid places, people and things that will lure you back into sexual sin.
- ◆ Be content with all that the Lord has given you.

Someone said "Sow a thought, reap an action, sow an action, reap a habit; sow a habit, reap a character; sow a character, reap a destiny". What are you sowing in your life today?

Sex and love are they the same?

Sex outside marriage is lust. The eye sight of lust is blind but that of true love is wide open. Sex and love are not and can never be the same. It is possible to have sex without love that is why there are professional prostitutes (harlots) like in *Judges 16:1-4*. Samson never loved the harlot; he slept with her but left her to the one he loved. Sisters, never buy love from any one with sex; it doesn't last nor pay. You are a child of the most High God; don't sell yourself. A man or woman who measures your love for him or her by demanding sex outside marriage from you is not worth your attention in the first place. Run away fast from such persons just as Joseph did when Portiphar's wife tried to seduce him. If Joseph had remained in Portiphar's house sleeping with his master's wife, he would have remained a slave, never to get to the position of the Prime Minister let alone cater for his extended family and household *(Genesis 39-41)*.

Please do not mortgage your future by having sex outside marriage, as there are spiritual implications and damage to one's relationship with God.

Once defiled, can I be made whole again?

Defiled here is used to mean having lost your virginity outside of your marriage. Defiling is not just in the physical but also more into the spiritual life of the person involved. Whilst the physical results may remain the same for life (e.g. once you lose your virginity no technology or medicine can make you a 100% virgin again), there can be a transformation of the spirit, mind and emotions by the blood of the Lamb. Giving your life to Christ and abiding in Him can make 'all things new' and make you a spiritual virgin.

Is it sinful or harmful to remain a virgin until my marriage?

It is not sinful or harmful in any way to remain a virgin till you are married. Your spouse, parents and children will in later years appreciate this virtuous gesture. It is said that of all of God's creation, only in the girl / woman is the hymen (the tissue that covers the entrance to the vagina of a virgin) seen.

Can I still be a virgin whilst practising oral or anal sex?

Whether oral, anal, or traditional sex, all are sex anyhow. There is always an exchange of some form of body fluid, which makes the people involved enter into a covenant relationship. Equally, as one thing leads to another, one form of sex will invariably trigger engaging in normal sexual intercourse. Delayed gratification in this matter is an important part of love and trust in the future. Why get involved in unedifying sexual acts when you can be happily married and enjoy sex as God ordained it?

SEX

Is masturbating safe or is it sinful?

First, masturbation is when a person stimulates his or her sexual organs to gain sexual satisfaction. It can best be described as having sex with one's self or gaining sexual satisfaction with one's self as when it is done with another person. It is not safe and it is sinful as it isn't God ordained and can become an addictive stronghold like doing drugs etc. Many Christians quietly practise masturbation because they feel it is better than having sexual intercourse with someone else but it usually leaves them living in guilt, it becomes difficult to overcome and much more difficult and embarrassing to be discussed at counselling. It may also be a stumbling block to having a meaningful lasting relationship with the opposite sex.

The good news is that like any other bondage or yoke, you can be set free from masturbation; it is a pardonable sin once you come clean before God. Go for counselling and strive to be accountable to a godly mature, sensitive Christian. You will also need to avoid things, places, people or situations that lure you back into this stronghold. Ask God to take the desire for it away from you.

Receive strength to resist temptation as you prayerfully meditate on the words of this song:

'Yield Not To Temptation'

Yield not to temptation, for yielding is sin;
Each victory will help you some other to win;
Fight manfully onward, dark passions subdue,
Look ever to Jesus, He'll carry you through.
Refrain
Ask the Saviour to help you,
Comfort, strengthen and keep you;
He is willing to aid you,
He will carry you through.

Shun evil companions, bad language disdain,
God's name hold in reverence, nor take it in vain;
Be thoughtful and earnest, kindhearted and true,
Look ever to Jesus, He'll carry you through.
Refrain

To him that o'ercometh, God giveth a crown;
Through faith we shall conquer, though often cast down;
He who is our Saviour our strength will renew;
Look ever to Jesus, He'll carry you through.
Refrain

Words and music written by Horatio R. Palmer (1868)
Source: Words and music on www.cyberhymnal.org/htm/y/i/yieldnot.htm

How to recognise and deal with sexual abuse

Sexual abuse is when a person is coerced to have sexual relationship of any type with someone else e.g. rape. This might be from another family member – father, mother, brother, sister, uncle, in-law, aunt, cousin, etc.

Having sex with a family member is called incest. Abuse may also be from a boy friend, sugar daddy or mummy, boss at work, school teacher, college lecturer, neighbour, pastor, elder or deacon in the Church, etc. Sometimes the abuse comes following threats, giving material gifts, making promises or initial show of care by the abuser.

In dealing with sexual abuse:

- Recognize it as sexual abuse and that it is not right for you to be defiled neither are you a toy to be played with or a sex slave, there to satisfy the urge of the 'master'. This is irrespective of the status or relationship of the abuser to you.
- Be aware that many abusers tend to want to blackmail their victims, convincing them that no one will believe their story, please don't believe this lie as out there are people who will believe you.
- If you can, expose the abuser to whoever can challenge

'Let's Reason Together ...Youths' A-Z

him or her e.g. parents, your teacher, pastor, doctor or the Police so long as they are not the perpetrators of the abuse.
- Run as far away as possible from the abuser to wherever will be safe or to whoever will believe your story enough to investigate it.
- Only confront abuser directly if it will not endanger you in the short term or long term otherwise, just apply any of the above that is most appropriate for you.
- Call on God to help you out of the mess.
- Never keep quiet, for sexual abuse can be very damaging. Seek for help as soon as possible. Don't be scared, there are people out there who will believe your story and get you out of the mess.

It is not uncommon for the one abused to feel guilty, dirty, unworthy, have low self esteem, etc. These are all lies of the devil. In the sight of God your creator, you have not lost any value, He still loves you, and if you allow Him into your world and situation He will make that painful experience work for your good and bring beauty out of your ashes. Just as crumpling or stepping on the largest denomination in your country's currency (e.g. £50 note in the UK, $100 in the USA, ₦1000 in Nigeria or washing it in the washing machine) does not reduce its monetary value afterwards, so having been abused does not remove your value before God.

An unexposed sexual abuser is as dangerous as a dog with rabies, free to attack and abuse another innocent victim unless exposed and stopped. Therefore, for the love of yourself and others do not keep quiet about your experience.

EXERCISE:

- ❖ All my unmarried friends are having sexual intercourse except me, am I abnormal?
- ❖ Is having sexual intercourse a sin?
- ❖ How do I show love or receive love if I refuse to engage in premarital sexual intercourse?
- ❖ It's my body after all, why should I refrain from premarital sex?
- ❖ Is it true that making love to a virgin is the cure for AIDS? NO!

PRAYER POINTS:

Lord, thank You for exposing Your truth and the lies of the enemy on this subject of sex.

Father, please help me to keep myself undefiled before You and please protect me from the wolves of this world.
Or
Father in ignorance, stubbornness and waywardness, I have been engaging in premarital sex. Do please forgive me, cleanse me heal my emotions from now on.

Lord, how I need Your help to live for You from now on in Jesus name.

*****The coordinator should spend quality time in dealing with this topic that has caused many to fall. You really don't have to finish the topic in one meeting. Also, please give room for confidential counselling and prayers at the end of the discussion. It is therefore important that both male and female youth coordinators are around when this topic is being discussed so that the man can counsel and follow up the males and vice versa. There are more useful addresses of where to get additional information and help at the end of this book.*

SOME SEXUAL ABUSE HELPLINES IN THE UK:
Off Record
Tel. Number 0208 251 0251

Face to face
Tel Number 0208 667 0207

Rape & Sexual Abuse Support
Tel. Number 0208 683 3311

The Shepherd's Ministries
5 Brookehowse Road
Bellingham
London SE6 3TJ, UK
Tel/Fax: +44 208 698 7222
Email: info@theshepherdsministries.org
Website: www.theshepherdsministries.org

Your local Social Services helpline should be able to direct you appropriately.

IN NIGERIA:

Children's Evangelism Ministry Inc
P.O. Box 4480
Ilorin, Kwara State,
Nigeria.
Tel: +234 31 222199
E-mail: cem@ilorin.skannet.com

Teenagers' Outreach Ministries
www.teenagersoutreachministries.Org.

IN USA:

www.eCounseling.com
Tel Number: 1-866-268-6735

Make a contact today if you or someone you know needs help. You are only a phone call away from freedom from sexual abuse.

SEX

TEMPTATIONS

"God, lead me not into temptation and deliver me from every evil."

"For no temptation (no trial regarded as enticing to sin), [no matter how it comes or where it leads] has overtaken you {and} laid hold on you that is not common to man [that is, no temptation or trial has come to you that is beyond human resistance and that is not adjusted and adapted and belonging to human experience, and such as man can bear]. But God is faithful [to His Word and to His compassionate nature], and He [can be trusted] not to let you be tempted {and} tried {and} assayed beyond your ability {and} strength of resistance {and} power to endure, but with the temptation He will [always] also provide the way out (the means of escape to a landing place), that you may be capable {and} strong {and} powerful to bear up under it patiently." [1 Corinthians 10:13].

Questions For Consideration/Discussion
1. What is temptation?
2. Why do we face temptations?
3. Who is the author of temptations?
4. How to deal with or overcome temptation.
5. Temptation and promotion are they related.

TEMPTATIONS

What is temptation?

It is mostly a set up by Satan to lure us to do things that are against God's will or plan for our lives. It is always a strong attraction for us to disobey God, hurt others, and even ourselves. Yielding to temptation ultimately means disobeying God, the consequences of which can be devastating both to the person and several generations to come. Temptation is a strong desire that can be mastered and tamed through the word of God and washing by the blood of Jesus.

Why do we face temptations?

God does not tempt us but He sometimes allows us to be tempted to prove the devil wrong; to help us really know our limits and define our boundaries; or to promote us once we successfully overcome the temptation.

Who is the author of temptations?

Satan, our flesh and the world, including ungodly friends and relations are sources of temptation. *(See Genesis 3; Matthew 4:1-11; Luke 4:1-13)*. Temptation most often comes up when we are alone, in a vulnerable condition (e.g. tired, hungry, weak, lonely, far from Church or away from the company of other believers), or where we cannot quickly get help or read the Bible. Jesus was led to the wilderness to be tempted.

How to deal with or overcome temptation

- ❖ Long before any temptation happens, resolve in your mind to always obey God, just like Daniel and his friends who purposed in their minds not to defile themselves with the king's food *(Daniel 1)*.
- ❖ Be disciplined and trust God to help you do His will only.
- ❖ Hide God's words in your heart *(Psalm 119:11)*.
- ❖ Reply the devil with the words of God like Jesus did *(Matthew 4)*.
- ❖ Realise that there is no short cut in life so don't listen to the lies of the enemy.
- ❖ Refuse to give in to temptation for your promotion is nearby.
- ❖ Be prayerful –Jesus said pray that you may not enter into temptation *(Matthew 26:41; Mark 14:38)*.
- ❖ Walk with God closely enough to differentiate His voice from that of the devil.

*When God speaks to us, His voice is often soft, and what He says will never contradict His will as contained in the

Bible. When the human flesh talks to us it will always want to satisfy itself instantly, wanting the easy way out not necessarily God's way out of the temptation. What the flesh will demand may be contrary to what the Spirit of God wants for us. Satan's voice is always against the will of God; it is forceful, harassing us to disobey God at every given opportunity.

Temptation and promotion are they related?

Just as someone said to be elevated you have to be separated, so it is often true that to be promoted you have to be tried or put through a test by God. Never expect to be used by God mightily until you have been tried and attained God's standard especially in the areas in which He plans to use you. Temptation is not always a one off event so we need to be careful and prayerful at all times.

EXERCISE:

- ◆ In what ways have you been tempted before?
- ◆ Where were you when you were tempted?
- ◆ What was your response to the temptation?
- ◆ Did you overcome the temptation or otherwise?
- ◆ What are you struggling with at present that the enemy may use to tempt you? E.g. talent, beauty, pride, malice, low self esteem, prayerlessness etc.

PRAYER POINTS:

Lord, I humbly confess the times that I have yielded to temptation in times past.

Father, in Your mercy please help me to be aware of the temptations that surround me daily.

Lord, please lead me not into temptation and deliver me from every known and unknown evil.

'Let's Reason Together ...Youths' A-Z

MY PERSONAL NOTES

UNBELIEF

"Unbelievers run from pillar to post while believers run from praise to power."

"But without faith it is impossible to please {and} be satisfactory to Him. For whoever would come near to God must [necessarily] believe that God exists and that He is the rewarder of those who earnestly {and} diligently seek Him [out]."
[Hebrews 11:6].

Question For Consideration/Discussion
1. What is unbelief?
2. Why do we have unbelief?
3. How is our unbelief exposed?
4. Examples of unbelief in the Bible.

What is unbelief?

Simply put, this means lack of faith in someone or something, non-belief, scepticism, incredulity, disbelief, agnosticism. For this discussion, we are looking at the sin of unbelief towards God i.e. not believing God.

Why do we have unbelief?

This is because we still have the nature of Adam in us, which makes us tend to find it easier to doubt rather than believe God. Unbelief could also be due to our lack of knowledge of God and our situation, or limitation of His power and ability. Some would argue that miracles are things of the past not for now, forgetting that the Bible says Jesus Christ is the same, yesterday, today and forever more.

How is our unbelief exposed?

Nothing exposes our unbelief faster than our confessions, expressions, actions and lack of actions. Imagine you have just prayed with your prayer partner for something e.g. healing in some part of your body. A few minutes later, someone asks you how you feel and you say "I feel awfully sick". That brief response just exposed your unbelief in

UNBELIEF

the prayers you said. Without faith in God we can receive nothing from Him *(Hebrews 11:6)*.

Examples of unbelief in the Bible

1. Eve disbelieved God and the penalty for her disobedience was a curse *(Genesis 3)*.
2. The people in the hometown of Jesus did not believe Him therefore He couldn't do many miracles there *(Matthew 13:54-58)*.
3. Thomas did not believe that Jesus had risen from the grave *(John 20:24-29)*.

** Apart from unbelief in God or in the Bible, unbelief can be seen too in the secular world. e.g. Despite documented potential medical damage to their bodies, many who do not belief that they can harm their body by how they disrespect and treat it may continue to smoke or do drugs, eat unhealthily, go into prostitution, etc.

EXERCISE:

❖ Identify areas of unbelief in your life.
❖ Why do you have unbelief?
❖ Knowledge, experience and unbelief – are they related?
❖ How can you overcome unbelief?

PRAYER POINTS:

Lord, please forgive me for all my unbelief in You and Your words.

Father, please help me overcome in the areas where I struggle with unbelief.

Lord, I believe in You and Your words, please help all my unbeliefs.

UNBELIEF

VISION

"My vision will affect my mission in life."

"Where there is no vision [no redemptive revelation of God], the people perish;" *[Proverbs 29:18]*

Questions For Consideration/Discussion
1. What is vision?
2. Why do I need to have a vision?
3. Vision and mission any relationship?
4. Examples of those who had a vision in the Bible.
5. Vision killers and vision helpers.

What is vision?

Vision could be an idea, a goal in life, image, foresight, revelation, mental picture, hallucination and apparition of something that has not come to pass yet. For many, vision is what stimulates them to want to keep going on in life in spite of all the oppositions and challenges they face. A vision could also be a dream or revelation from God.

Why do I need to have a vision?

Properly channelled and utilised, a vision can change a beggar to the most wealthy man in town. A properly executed vision could save lives, bless many others and help to prevent loss of life and property.

Vision and mission any relationship?

Without a vision there can be no mission. Unless you know where you are going in life or what you want to do, you may pass it many times without realising it. As the eyes are to the body, so is vision to a mission. The power of vision is so strong that God told Abraham that as much as he could see would be given to him *(Genesis 13:14-18)*. Your vision

VISION

will affect your thinking and what you can see in the Spirit is what you are likely to get in the physical realm.

Examples of those who had a vision in the Bible:
- Abraham *(Genesis 12:1-3).*
- Jacob at Bethel *(Genesis 28:10-22).*
- Joseph *(Genesis 37).*
- Moses *(Exodus 3).*
- Joseph the husband of Mary *(Matthew 1:18 – 2:23).*

Vision killers and helpers

Anything or anyone that wants to undermine or destroy your dream, God's revelation to you previously or currently is a vision killer and anything or anyone who seeks to enhance your vision is a vision helper. *(Not arranged in a particular order:)*

Vision killers	Vision Helpers
Sin	Obedience to God and His word.

'Let's Reason Together ...Youths' A-Z

Fear	Faith in God that He is able to bring the vision to come to pass. Faith in yourself that with God all things are possible for you to achieve.
Ungodly companions	Godly companions.
Ingratitude	Grateful attitude.
Murmuring and complaining	Fellowship with God all the time.
Satan	Holy Spirit.
Anyone whose relationship with you diminishes or demeans your vision.	Anyone whose relationship with you enhances your vision.

EXERCISE:

❖ Identify your vision and mission.
❖ What do you need for your vision to be fulfilled?
❖ How can you make your vision become reality?
❖ What impact do you want to make in life?
❖ Praying for my vision. Is that really necessary?

PRAYER POINTS:

Lord, please give me a clear vision of my calling in life.

Father, in Your mercy, please deliver me from all forms of vision killers and destiny terminators..

Lord, please send me a vision helper in Jesus name.

VISION

WORDS

"What I call forth will come forth."

"A good man eats good from the fruit of his mouth, but the desire of the treacherous is for violence." [Proverbs 13:2].

Questions for Consideration/Discussion
1. What are words ?
2. Types of words,
3. Who speaks to you?
4. Why do you need to use words?
5. Words and their effects.

What are words?

Words could be an expression, a language, writing, verbal skill used to communicate our feelings, needs, desires or actions to others.. A person's words define him or her. Words are generally spoken from the abundance of what is in one's heart, which in turn is influenced by what we hear, what we see, where we have been, what we have experienced, the company we keep and family background.

Types of words

Words could either be spoken or written. Both have the same and equal value.

Who speaks to you?

God speaks to us. Man or self also speaks and Satan is able to speak too if we allow him.

Why do you need to use words?

We use words to express our feelings, needs, desires, opinions etc. Communication can be verbal or non verbal. In verbal communication, the use of words is mandatory. Even God did not do anything without speaking it first *(Genesis 1)*. Every miracle Jesus Christ performed whilst on earth was preceded by His spoken words. Our words reflect who we are, whose we are and what is in our hearts. To speak like our Father God, we ought to learn to renew our minds daily with His words as contained in the Bible.

Words and their effects

God's words are sovereign and so will not return to Him void *(Isaiah 55: 10-11)*. Our words are equally powerful and do not die. They attract negative or positive aura once they are spoken. For example the oil flow stopped the minute the widow's son said there were no more containers *(2 Kings 4: 1-7)*. In another story, the Shunammite woman refused to give up on her dead son by her actions and confession that "It is well" and indeed the dead boy was raised to life by Prophet Elisha *(2 Kings 4: 8-37)*. Twelve men were sent to spy the Promised Land; ten returned to say they were not able to defeat the giants there and God made sure they died in the wilderness without entering Canaan. The remaining two that said they were well able to defeat the giants in Canaan were the only ones in their generation that indeed got into the Promised Land *(Numbers 13-14, 26:64-65)*. What have you been saying about your life, situation, circumstances or family? We need to watch the words we use for others and for ourselves; we need to cancel immediately any negative words spoken to us or to our loved ones irrespective of who spoke them.

EXERCISE:

❖ How would you rate your words (wise, soothing, uplifting or otherwise)?
❖ How much of God's words do you know for yourself?
❖ What are the words of the music you listen to?
❖ God will judge every careless word. True or false?
❖ What or who has been influencing your words (friends, family, drugs, drinks etc)?
❖ How do you overcome words that get you in trouble?
❖ Your words and yourself are they separable? Why or why not?

PRAYER POINTS:

Lord, please forgive me for saying the wrong things especially in the heat of my troubles/ struggles.

Father, please help me to fill my heart and mind with Your words alone.

Lord, please help me to speak helpful and useful words only knowing that I shall stand before You one day to account for all my words.

'Let's Reason Together ...Youths' A-Z

MY PERSONAL NOTES

X - RAY

"As an X-ray reveals the body parts so God sees through my spirit, motives and actions."

"Search me [thoroughly], O God, and know my heart! Try me and know my thoughts! And see if there is any wicked {or} hurtful way in me, and lead me in the way everlasting."
[Psalm 139:23-24].

Questions for Consideration/ Discussion:
1. What is an X- ray?
2. Why do some people need an X-ray examination?
3. What is the difference between an X-ray image and an outward photograph?
4. What is seeing through the human mind?

What is an X-ray?

It means electromagnetic-radiation that is used in imaging the bones and inside the body of people.

Why do some people need an X-ray examination?

An X-ray examination might become necessary to confirm or refute broken bones or body parts, to assess the functioning of some organs with the use of contrast medium, to determine the extent of a disease, to assess the normality of the anatomy of some body parts or organs, and to monitor treatment progress or regress.

What is the difference between an X-ray image and an outward photograph?

	X-RAY	OUTWARD PHOTOGRAPH
1.	Shows inner anatomy of the person	Shows outward appearance only.
2.	You can't dress up a person's inside to look good or bad when it isn't really so.	Can dress up and pretend all is well or otherwise when it isn't.

3.	Needs experts to take image and interpret the image (s)	Seen and understood by everybody.
4.	Needs special equipment	Does not need special equipment.
5.	Equipment used not accessible to the public (i.e. available only in hospitals and medical centres).	Photographic cameras are available to the public.

Seeing through the human mind:

Unlike X-radiation, God can see what is inside the heart of everyone, everywhere and every time yet, He is not confused and cannot be deceived. He can 'see' what you are thinking; He knows your motives even when you try to justify your actions. God listens to every conversation, every whisper, every unspoken word and every unuttered desire and want. What makes this beautiful is that God doesn't misunderstand you no matter what. He understands every language and hears every cry to Him for help. God hears all praises too.

While an X-ray examination can reveal some anatomy and function of the body parts, only God can make every body part to work properly; only God can effect a positive change in them.

Human nature thinks evil at every opportunity therefore, we need to daily, moment by moment, renew our mind with the word of God. Our thoughts will invariably influence our actions.

Prayerfully meditate on this song:
Purify my heart
Let me be as gold
And precious silver
Purify my heart
Let me be as gold
Pure gold

Refiner's fire
My heart's one desire
Is to be holy
Set apart for You, Lord
I choose to be holy
Set apart for You, my Master
Ready to do Your will

XENOPHOBIA

*Purify my heart
Cleanse me from within
And make me holy
Purify my heart
Cleanse me from my sin
Deep within*

*© 1990 Mercy/Vineyard Publishing Purify my heart
Source: http://www.audiblefaith.com/pages/sg853379*

EXERCISE:

- ❖ How can you know all that is in your heart?
- ❖ Is your heart clean or dirty?
- ❖ God is a silent listener to every conversation. True or false?
- ❖ What proofs do you have for the answer you gave above?
- ❖ God knows all that is on my mind. True or false? Why do you say so?

PRAYER POINTS:

Lord, please reveal to me what is in my heart and life.

Fathe,r please purify my heart and thoughts to Your will only.

Lord, help me to meditate on You and Your words moment by moment of each day.

'Let's Reason Together ...Youths' A-Z

MY PERSONAL NOTES

YOUTH

YOUTH

"I will remember now my Creator in the days of my youth."

"Let no one despise {or} think less of you because of your youth, but be an example (pattern) for the believers in speech, in conduct, in love, in faith, and in purity." [1 Timothy 4:12].

Questions for Consideration/Discussion
1. What is it to be a youth?
2. What makes the youth peculiar?
3. Youths and their hormones.
4. Youths and their actions.
5. Youths and church attendance today
6. Youths and alternative religion.
7. Youths and their parents.
8. Does God use youths?

What is it to be a youth?

The word youth is associated with a period of adolescence, puberty, teenage years, and early stages of adulthood.

What makes the youth peculiar?

Under normal circumstances, youths are naturally full of energy, full of life, experience visible rapid growth changes, and are very daring in their recreation. Often times, they are in search of knowledge of what life is all about, who they are, and as their consciousness increases Mum or Dad might not be their choice of confidants as before. For those not watching their weight, their regular visits to the kitchen tell what they have been there for.

Youths and their hormones

At this stage there are many hormones circulating within their system, some of which help in their sexual development. Hormonal changes may also cause youths to experience mood swings. Like someone has put it, boys and girls are half way between being children and becoming full adults in their teenage years. Height and size often rapidly increase. They feel they are capable of making their own decisions and may decline help from relatives.

Youths and their actions

Many youths do not sit down and to weigh their intended action so they get into trouble that could have been averted. Some have abandoned the Christian faith of their parents. Some think life is just a big joke or an experiment in their actions. They forget that for every action there is a resulting reward.

Youth and church attendance today

There is the tendency for some youths to feel that because they were forced to attend Sunday School when they were younger they can make up their mind now if to attend Church or not. Some say the Church is irrelevant to them. Unfortunately, this may be true in some Churches where the youths are not given enough spiritual or physical challenges to occupy them and not much attention is given to their personal problems.

Youths and alternative religion

Many are trying alternative religion to fill the void in their life but the solution lies /lays in only one person – Jesus Christ. Many alternative religions are occultic and demonic, exposing their followers to more dangers and complications. There is no true peace and joy outside of Jesus Christ.

Youths and their parents

Unless prayerfully addressed, this period could turn out to be a time for unplanned crisis within the family. The Bible commands young people to obey their parents and that is the first commandment with a blessing *(Exodus 20:12; Ephesians 6:1-3)*. Most parents under normal circumstances want the best for their children but often times the best is not communicated appropriately. Parental questioning could be due to curiosity about the subject of discussion, or lack of trust of the child and vice versa. Discussion and dialogue at appropriate moments could be very helpful in such circumstances. It is important to say too that fathers should not provoke their children to wrath: but bring them up in the nurture and admonition of the Lord *(Ephesians 6:4)*.

Does God use youths?

Yes He does and will if the young person allows Him to. God used the maid of Naaman's wife to get Naaman healed; He anointed David so that he killed Goliath as a youth. Daniel was a youth when he was selected amongst others to be trained in a foreign land and language for royal duties. Timothy was a youth when Paul chose Him to be a Church leader. God is able and willing to bless you and use you even much better than you can imagine.

EXERCISE:

- ◈ Search your Bible for the scriptural references of the examples given in the discussion above of youths that God used.
- ◈ Why are youths generally misunderstood?
- ◈ Why must youths be obedient to their parents and other positive authority?
- ◈ Youth and loud music, youth and parties. Is anything wrong?
- ◈ Is there a place for today's youth in the Church, home or society?
- ◈ Youth and physical challenges, where do I draw the line?
- ◈ What do you as a youth expect from yourself, parents, Church and community?

PRAYER POINTS:

Lord, thank You for keeping me safe as a youth.

Father, please help that I will not be derailed as a young person. Do please order my steps and stops in life as from now in Jesus name.

Lord, please help me to be conscious of my growth both spiritually, physically and in other other ways.

'Let's Reason Together ...Youths' A-Z

MY PERSONAL NOTES

ZEAL

"The zeal of the Lord is upon me."

"... and [consequently] your enthusiasm has stimulated the majority of them." [2 Corinthians 9:2b].

Questions for Consideration/Discussion
1. What is zeal?
2. What is your zeal for?
3. Effects of your zeal on yourself and others.

What is zeal?

This means passion, commitment, eagerness, keenness, fanaticism, enthusiasm, fervour or ardour for something or someone.

What is your zeal for?

Would you say what you have a passion that will glorify God or otherwise? Hidden in your zeal or passion might be your life assignment. However, to become all that God has planned for you, you will need to submit your zeal to Him and be trained by Him even if the timing and method may be frightening and long by human standards. My zeal is in sharing my God-given knowledge and experience through writing but it has taken over fifteen years of all forms of training and challenges to get to this stage. I am even now still undergoing God's training!

Effects of your zeal on yourself and others

Whatever we do affects others around us directly or indirectly. Paul, formerly known as Saul was very zealous but it was a wrongly directed zeal until God met with him and he became a Christian. Paul's zeal was now redirected to preaching the Gospel with the same passion he was formerly using to stop its spread *(Acts 9:1-31)*. There is no one that God cannot change. There is no useless talent or person. We just need to discover where and how the talent could best be used to glorify God and bless His people.

EXERCISE:

◈ Identify your zeal.
◈ How did you develop a zeal for that thing?
◈ How committed are you to that which you have a zeal for?
◈ How can you use your zeal for God?
◈ How can you and others benefit from your zeal?
◈ What price have you paid or are you willing to pay to pursue that zeal in you?

PRAYER POINTS:

Lord, please help me to identify my zeal in life.

Father, may You please lead me to where and to those who will help me develop and enhance my zeal.

Lord, thank You for blessing me as I worked through this book.

ZEAL

Summary

A **Anger**
"Anger is one letter short of danger."

B **Betrayal/backstabbing**
"Betrayal/backstabbing is wickedness."

C **Contentment**
"A contented life is a protected life."

D **Drugs**
"I refuse to defile my body with drugs."

E **Examination**
"Examination is the pathway to promotion."

F **Faith**
"It is impossible for me to please God without faith."

G **Growth**
"I must read my Bible and pray everyday in order for me to grow."

H **Homosexuality**
"God's ordained sexual love is between a man and a woman."

I **Ignorance**
"All ignorance gets paid for."

J **Jealousy**
"Negative jealousy opens me up to lack of peace."

K **Kindness**
"Kindness is being good to your fellow men."

'Let's Reason Together ...Youths' A-Z

L **Lawful**
"*Lawful does not mean helpful or useful.*"

M **Money**
"*My worth is not in the money I have or don't have.*"

N **Name**
"*A good name is far better than riches.*"

O **Obedience**
"*It pays to be obedient.*"

P **Praise**
"*I am alive therefore I will praise the Lord.*"

Q **Quiet time**
"*Prayer is the master key to every situation in life.*"

R **Rejection**
"*I am special to God and He will never reject me.*"

S **Sex**
"*With God's help I will keep my marriage bed undefiled.*"

T **Temptation**
"*God, lead me not into temptation and deliver me from every evil.*"

U **Unbelief**
"*Unbelievers runs from pillar to post while believers run from praise to power.*"

V **Vision**
"*My vision will affect my mission in life.*"

W **Words**
"*What I call forth will come forth.*"

X **X-Ray**
"As an X-ray reveals the body parts, so God sees through my spirit, motives and actions."

Y **Youth**
"I will remember now my Creator in the days of my youth."

Z **Zeal**
"The zeal of the Lord is upon me."

IT'S MY LIFE

'It's my life' you say and you are correct
'I can live just the way I want and choose'
Sleeping all day instead of going to school or work
Watching the television twenty-four seven
Staying on the 'dole' instead of seeking for employment
Partying, clubbing instead of studying or working
Sleeping around with whomever and whenever
Instead of keeping your body a temple for God
Overeating instead of eating moderately
Overworking instead of taking adequate rest
It's my life you keep saying to yourself and others.

'It's my life' you say and you are correct
Friend, remember it is indeed your life
Once you choose your behaviour
You have chosen the reward of your behaviour
Time now to reconsider, time now to re-think

'Let's Reason Together ...Youths' A-Z

For you have just one life
Why end up in pain and shame?
Why live in abject poverty and starve,
When God has a better place and plan for you?
It's your life so make the best of it friend.

O.Ola-Ojo 14.06.08

MY FAITH IS BEING PUT TO TEST.

Many times in life I do not understand
Why I have to pass through difficult times
Sometimes having to work with difficult people
Sometimes having to live with difficult people
Sometimes having to have difficult experiences
But like the man of God rightly mentioned
My faith is being put to test through them all.

I may not be able to explain to anyone
What pains I have suffered in this life
What trials and difficulties I have gone through
What hardships I have faced as a person
What burdens have remained unburdened?
What temptations I have been subjected to
As my faith is being put to test in all.

*I perfectly admit how I feel all these while
I personally confess how I feel like at such times
I happily admit God's goodness even in them
I totally refuse to condemn You Lord or myself
I knowingly believe in Your love and faithfulness
I absolutely put my total confidence in You alone
As my faith is constantly being put to test.*

*I am going to allow God alone to have His way
To make the best of all these situations
To grant me enough grace to sail through
Or to transform the situations to His Glory
No matter how soon or how late God may be
To come to my aid in all these respects I believe
My own situation is never helpless or hopeless.*

Psalms 56: 2-4, 9b - 11. Ola - Ojo '89.

POEMS

NO CARELESS WORD.

Many words are spoken
At different places, to different people
By different authorities of different powers.

Some words are carelessly spoken
Others are spoken without thought
Worse still are those spoken with no intention of fulfilment.

Some words are carefully chosen
With thought and weight
Realising how important words could be.

Many leaders and politicians
Have made unrealistic, unreasonable promises
Knowing fully well that such cannot be kept.

Leaders and parents
Have made promises believing they could fulfil them
But fail as the circumstances get beyond their control .

'Let's Reason Together ...Youths' A-Z

*Some parents have spoken to their children
Promising them what they can never afford to give
Promises that have had the children's hopes dashed to the walls.*

*God's words are never carelessly spoken
Whether directly to an individual, a group or nation
Whether through the written words or prophetic messages.*

*His words will certainly come to pass
Irrespective of the time, place and people concerned
Regardless of the prevailing circumstances.*

*No careless word from the Almighty God
He means every word written or spoken
He watches His words and brings them to pass.*

*No careless word from the All knowing God.
Whether words of punishment or justice
Or words of healing, blessing or anointing*

*Over and over again He confirms His words
In the lives of His people
At His own appointed time and place.*

POEMS

Friend has God spoken to you now or before?
It will certainly come to pass, as God speaks no careless word.
Relax and be assured God speaks no careless word.
O. Ola - Ojo '91. Isaiah 55: 10 -11, Psalms 12:6.

'Let's Reason Together ...Youths' A-Z

THE DEAD END

It starts like any other road
It looks beautiful and attractive
Promising at the beginning
With signs to a destination.

What an unfortunate mistake to travel on it
What seemed attractive and beautiful
Unending and everlasting
Turns out to be one dead end.

Every sin dear friend is a dead end
For in the end it is full of disgrace and regrets
Full of heartaches, uncertainty and hatred
Full of bitterness, pity and unaccountable loss.

No matter how small or big that sin is
No matter where, when and how it was committed
No matter whatever excuse we might want to give
It does not remove the sin from being a dead end.

POEMS

Now is the time to retrace back your steps
Now is the time to reassess the situation again
Now is the time to seek the Lord's face once more
In order not to end up in the dead end.

The dead end has nothing to offer
It has no guarantee, no security nor peace
It has no degree of commitment or improvement
It has no hope for a better future.

In your daily walk in life
Do try and watch out for dead ends
Do not be attracted to it or trapped in it
For in the end it is going to be what it is, the dead end.
© O.Ola–Ojo 11.03.92.

'Let's Reason Together ...Youths' A-Z

YOU ARE NOT ALONE

Do you sometimes feel you can no longer cope with life?
Do you sometimes feel hungry even after a supposed good meal?
Do you sometimes get angry with yourself over small things?
Do you sometimes feel lonely and lost amidst the greatest crowd?

Do you at times feel you cannot sincerely understand yourself?
Do you many times wish you were never born into this world?
Do you feel helpless about many situations you cannot change?
Do you find people many times misinterpreting your good intentions?

Do you feel unfulfilled despite your reputable status?
Do you feel unloved by your family and very close friends?
Do you suffer from unrealised hopes and dreams beloved?
*Do you think you need an immediate change for bette*r*?*

Dear friend you are not alone in that very feeling of yours
You are not alone in that seemingly difficult situation
You are not alone right now wherever you may be in this world
Cheer up for feelings are many times like the weather

POEMS

Subject to a change for better only by Divine Intervention
Unknowing to you many people are in similar or worst situations
Look around where you are now and be reassured that you are not alone
Your situation can change for better in a split of a fraction of a second.

Jesus Christ is there with you ready to make the desired change
He is waiting and wanting to help if you will ask Him
For God's wish for your feelings, longings and emotions
Is to make them work eventually for your own very good

© Ola-Ojo Based on Rom.8: 28. Written on 23/3/92

AT LIFE'S EDGE

Failure in life sometimes is not limited to the weak and unprepared
Experienced and brilliant people sometimes fail too
In spite of their hard work, experience, abilities and intelligence
It must be so painful and stressful not to have anything to show for it.

Simon Peter and his friends have been fishing all through the night
They were professional fishermen who understood their trade
They toiled all night in the dark and coldness on the sea
They caught nothing by morning, what a wasted effort!

At the edge of the waters stood their boats as they mended their nets
In their tiredness and weariness they prepared for the next day
Close by on the seashore a great crowd had gathered and possibly watching

POEMS

For Jesus was there preaching on the shore of that very lake.
They must have been disappointed and frustrated by their failure
At the water's edge they had stood their boats that were empty
They were engrossed in the washing and mending of their nets
Joining the crowd to listen to Jesus was not for them at that moment.

Noticing the two empty boats at the edge of the water
Jesus stepped into one of them and asked Simon the owner
for a push
Out a little into the waters so He could sit in it and preach
to the crowd
Who had been earlier pressing on Him to here the Word of God.

Friend you too today may be at life's edge frustrated at
your failure
Your boats are empty and you are mending and washing your
professional tools
You have nothing to show for your hard work and midnight toils
And what more there is a great crowd around possibly watching.

At life's edge of problems and failures you are standing
Your experience, expertise, formulas and input has failed you
You are exhausted, tired and possibly fed up with everything
Friend, don't despair as God is about to bring about your
miracle.

'Let's Reason Together ...Youths' A-Z

You are too possibly engrossed in your failures, tired and weary
Another stress could possibly give you a complete breakdown
Too sad to join the crowds whatever the cause of their gathering
Too busy mending and minding your own business and life.

Jesus is there, right there at your life's edge beloved
You are so special that He wants to come right into your situation
Not only to sort you out but equally to use and bless you
Your empty boat to fill to overflowing dearly beloved.

At life's edge God is going to meet you and speak to you
A response and demand He will expect from you
A change beyond your expectation and understanding will occur
Failures will be turned to fruitfulness as you faithfully obey Him.

As He calls you out among others in front of the crowd
Not only to get your attention but to ask for that empty boat
Asking that you once again try in that in which you once have failed
Not to ridicule you in front of the crowd but to bless you abundantly.

©O.Ola-Ojo 10/10/93 Luke.5: 1-11

OPPORTUNITY TO BECOME A CHRISTIAN

Dear Father in heaven,

Thank you for the privilege of reading this book. Indeed I have sinned and come short of Your glory. I am grateful to You for sending Jesus Christ into this world to come to die on the cross of Calvary for me. I believe in my heart that Jesus Christ paid for my sins, past, present and future. I believe Jesus Christ was buried and on the third day He rose from the dead. I believe that Jesus Christ will come back again. I confess with my mouth and I accept Him now to be my Lord.

Master, Saviour, Brother, and Friend, I ask in Your mercy for the infilling of the Holy Spirit so that with His help, I can live a victorious life becoming all that You have ordained me to be in Jesus' name. I pray with thanksgiving. Amen.

If after reading this book you said the above prayer and became born-again, Congratulations! You are Born Again is a booklet for those who have done so through reading this book. It is a free booklet that we would like you to have. In it, the frequently asked questions are answered and this will get you on the way to growing in your newfound faith in God. You can download this free booklet from our website: www.protokospublishers.com

You may also contact any of the organisations listed at the end of the book.

I look forward to hearing from you soon.
O. Ola-Ojo (2010)

Other Books By The Author:

Provocation, Prayer and Praise
(December 2004 & 2009)

Complimentary to The Christian and Infertility this book focuses on the story of an infertile woman in the Bible, her provocations, prayer and praise. Whatever makes you incomplete, unfulfilled, less than whom God made you to be, whatever issue of life that the enemy uses to provoke you calls for prayer.

Key features include:
- Some known medical reasons for infertility in the women.
- Why Hannah went to the house of God in spite of her barrenness.
- Is it true that the husband is much more than 10 sons to the infertile woman?
- When, where and how to address the source/cause of your provocation.
- God's part and your part in that promise.
- God is able to met that humanly impossible need of yours.
- A time to celebrate and praise God.

Book Details:
Paperback: 128 pages
Language English
ISBN-13: 978-0-9557898-3-0

A Reader from London, 7 Jan 2006 on Amazon.co.uk
An excellent easy to read and understand book. The principles shared in this book though primarily are for those trying for a baby could as well be applied to any area of hurt and un-fulfilment.

 :www.protokospublishers.com

OTHER BOOKS

The Christian and Infertility
(December 2004 & 2009)

The Christian and Infertility addresses one of the often neglected needs of Christian couples. It gives an insight into infertility from the biblical and medical perspectives. It is written not only for potential fruitful couples but for pastors, family and friends of these couples. It is written that the Body of Christ might be fully equipped to know and support couples who are facing the challenge of infertility at present.

Key features include:
- Childleness in the Bible and lessons to learn;
- Some possible physical, medical and environmental causes of infertility;
- Some known spiritual causes of infertility;
- The man and low sperm count;
- Some of the available treatment optons in the UK;
- Choice of fertility treatment;
- Should a christian professional be involved in fertility treatment?

Book Details:
Paperback: 146 pages
Language English
ISBN-13: 978-0-9557898-2-3

A reviewer from Glen Burnie, USA, 29 Oct 2007 on Amazon.co.uk'
The book is a great eye-opener for all. It sheds light on infertility from the medical and spiritual angle. This gives the reader a balance because i believe every human being is made up of both physical and spiritual part. To get a balance in life, the two parts must be well fed. One must not concentrate on the spiritual and neglect the physical part. The book also reminds us that God has a way of sorting us out.... The book is quite inspiring. I will recommend this book to everybody trusting God for any form of blessing from God to go get one and apply it to his or her situation. It will definitely bless you and yours'.

 :www.protokospublishers.com

OTHER BOOKS

Obstetrics and Gynaecology Ultrasound -
A Self-Assessment Guide
June 2005 Churchill Elsevier Publishers, UK.

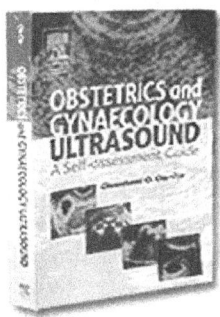

This self-assessment guide is a structured questions and answer book that develops the reader's understanding capability using a simple method in treating related topics. Clinical indications are presented with their corresponding ultrasound findings using appropriate illustrations. A case study approach is followed; presenting the clinical and ethical dilemmas that might arise whilst encouraging students to think. The aim is to reinforce theoretical knowledge within a clinical environment.

Key features:
- Over 600 high-resolution ultrasound images
- Cover a wide spectrum of ultrasound curriculum.
- Includes a detailed study of fertility.
- Aids quick understanding of subject matter.
- 468 pages.

ISBN-10: 0443064628
ISBN-13: 978-0443064623
Book Dimensions: 24 x 16.8 x 2.6 cm

"...This excellent new book is a study guide... This is an attractive paperback that should be essential reading for trainee obstetric and gynaecological sonographers, whether they are radiographers or radiology or obstetric trainees. It will be of particular value to those preparing for the RCOG/RCR Diploma in Advanced Obstetric Ultrasound and to specialist registrars in obstetrics and gynaecology undertaking special skills modules in fetal medicine, gynaecological ultrasound and infertility..."

The Obstetrician & Gynaecologist, www.rcog.org.uk/togonline
Book reviews 2006

Reviewer **Ann Harper MD FRCPI FRCOG.**
Consultant Obstetrician and Gynaecologist
Royal Jubilee Maternity Service, Belfast., UK

 :www.protokospublishers.com

OTHER BOOKS

GOOD MUMS, BAD MUMS
(June 2005 & 2009)

This is in two parts, the main chapter that can be used for personal or group study, and an accompanying exercise section. The privileged position of a mother is in her being a co-creator with God and bringing forth life (lives). This book compliments one of God's previous revelations to me as contained in the book titled Good Dads, Bad Dads'. While the father could be likened to the pilot of the family plane, the mother can be likened to the force behind the plane – positive or negative. Good mothers are not only co-creators with God, they also do nurture as well as nourish their children physically, emotionally and spiritually.

Keys Features:
- Were all the mothers in the Bible god mothers?
- Lessons from the strengths and weakness of seven mothers.
- Be encouraged - you are not alone in the assignment of motherhood.
- Be motivated in the areas of your strengths.
- Learn ways of supporting your husband and children.

Book Details:
Paperback: 162 pages
Language English
ISBN-13: 978-0-9557898-1-6
Book Dimensions: 21.4 x 14 x 1.4 cm

I appreciate the author's method of writing. It is always exciting holding her book to read. Personally, 'Good Mums, Bad Mums' has been a blessing to me in no small measure. The book is rich, it is loaded with physical and spiritual uplifting subjects. To all existing and potential mothers, this book is a MUST read. At the end of every chapter there is an exercise to do that will help in re-examining your life spiritually and in other ways. I encourage all women to get and use this book as a guide in raising their children. You will be glad you did.

Pastor Mrs T Adegoke
Freedom Arena
London, UK

 :www.protokospublishers.com

OTHER BOOKS

To the Bride with Love
(2007 & 2009)

Every wise woman preparing to get married knows she will need sound advice, practical tips and solid, heartfelt prayers, of those who have travelled on the road she is about to journey on. In this book, 10 women of different age groups, from different backgrounds and cultures who wedded under various circumstances, individually share their experience with the bride in an intimate, very candid and unforgettable way.

Book details:
Paperback: 108 pages
Language English
ISBN-13: 978-0-9557898-4-7
Book Dimensions: 22.4 x 15 x 1 cm

To the Bride with Love is the perfect bride's evergreen companion. The content is suitable, relevant and applicable even decades after the wedding day.

To the Bride with Love is an ideal wedding gift on its own. It can also accompany any other gift (big or small) that you have for the bride but take this hint... the bride will keep thanking you for the book years and years after.

'One of the best', 19 Jul 2008 on Amazon.com
Sade Olaoye "clare4good" (United Kingdom)
This book has really helped my marriage from the onset as I got it as a wedding gift, God bless the giver. It's a must read for relationship improvement and God's guidance. I recommend it for people to get it for themselves, moreover as a great blessing for someone else in love. "To the Bride with Love"

Review by **Oyinlola Odunlami** CEO.
Shallom Bookshop, London UK
The writing style of Oluwakemi is unique, peculiar and distinct to herself. I recommend To the Bride with Love to wives, wives to be, mothers, mentors, youth leaders and workers. Why? The clarity, the focus and the intent of this book is so empowering, encouraging and enlightening that it will definitely mould or re mould a life to achieve its purpose. The truth is, there are very few

OTHER BOOKS

books that have depth as well as help you to achieve your goals and arrive at your destination. Many books tend to excite you but have no depth; you read and you forget; they do not really change you but this book, To the Bride with Love will definitely leave a word in your spirit and move you to your next level!

I believe that this is also a book that pastors will find useful as a manual for marriage counselling, because many books on marriage focus mostly on what you as an individual can gain, your own personal satisfaction while little is said about the sacrifices involved and their importance. As my pastor usually says, it is important to learn from those who have gone ahead, understand why some were successful and others weren't, so that we won't fall where they fell, rather, we would gain more speed, achieve our goals and thereby glorify Christ.

So, I invite you not only to get a copy of this life-changing manual for yourself, but also to put it into as many hands as you can afford to, for then the world will definitely benefit and your life will be a blessing to many.

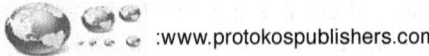
:www.protokospublishers.com

OTHER BOOKS

Refuge Under His Wings

"an exhaustive analysis of the Book of Ruth in the Bible. The author combines her deep Christian conviction and excellent knowledge of the Holy Scriptures to produce a must read for every Christian, married or single. The book is interspaced with beautifully written prayers, which enables the reader to pause, pray and meditate on the revelations received... The book is also loaded with poetry like 'Thy will be done oh Lord' for those who may be facing an uncertain future or on a cross road of decisions."

Dr E B Ekpo MD, FRCP
Queen Elizabeth Hospital, Christian Fellowship,
Woolwich, London. UK

"...[a] ...spiritually sound book... a fine work of thoughtful reading and study... I therefore recommend it to every Christian, married or single....
Pat Roach Senior Pastor
New Covenant Church.
Wandsworth Branch, London. UK.

Book details:
Paperback: 100 pages
Language English
ISBN-10: 095578980X
ISBN-13: 978-0955789809

This book feeds the soul. Most of all I loved the poetry. It gives you time to savour the thoughts as reader. There is a good mix of poetry and prose.To look at the story of Ruth in depth gave good spiritual food. You can pause and take it in at your own pace.The meditation on Psalm 121 was good also. There's nothing like reading a Psalm slowly and meditating on its contents. The author's own reflections allow you to see the book through someone else's eyes. A good read.

Book Review: by Gaby Richards, London, UK.

 :www.protokospublishers.com

OTHER BOOKS

GRACE OR WORKS

This book makes you examine a lot of issues in your life, family relationships in particular, that you may have taken for granted or totally ignored. As conveyed right from the rhetorical question posed in the title, Grace or Works, the author stirs you towards asking yourself pertinent questions, thinking through for answers and even getting solutions for unresolved problems.

Have you heard of prodigal wives, husbands, mothers or prodigal fathers? This book identifies and defines them clearly. For anyone experiencing a crises in their relationship with such prodigal family members, this book, which is based on the parable of the "Prodigal son" in Luke 15:11-32 is a one-stop resource material to meet your counselling needs. And just in case you happen to be the prodigal who has caused your relatives much sorrow, there is hope for you in this book.

Interspersed with prayers for you by the author and specific prayers that you can say for yourself, as well as poems to comfort and inspire you, Grace or Works not only asks you questions, it helps you make and maintain the right choices.

Book details:
Paperback: 122 pages
Language English
ISBN-13: 978-0-9557898-5-4

:www.protokospublishers.com

OTHER BOOKS

THERE IS A REWARD FOR PARENTING

Man may claim that the conception of a particular child was accidental, but in God's eyes every child is in His plan and has a purpose and mission to fulfil here on earth. As a parent, teacher, church or community leader, how are you treating the children in your care?

God does not sleep nor slumber; are you sure you are doing what He expects of you as a parent or children's Sunday school teacher? What kind of reward do you expect from Him?

There is a Reward for Parenting provides a lot of answers and food for thought, using scriptural principles to show you how to ensure a good reward from God in the unique assignment of parenting and child care.

As characteristic of Oluwakemi Ola-Ojo's previous books, there is a free gift of her poems at the end of this book also, to add value to the content of the main text – making it two books for the price of one!

Book details:
Paperback: 88 pages
Language English
ISBN 978-0-9557898-6-1

:www.protokospublishers.com

OTHER BOOKS

Let's Reason Together ...Youths' A-Z

According to the United Nations demographic statistics, the global youth population, ranging in age from 15 to 24 years, today stands at more than 1.5 billion, representing about 22 percent or a fifth of the world's 6.8 billion people inhabiting the earth. In developing nations where a greater number of this group resides, the youth population sometimes gets as high as 60% or more of the total population of such nations!

Since it is also globally accepted that the youth of any nation forms the strength of that nation, economically, militarily and/or otherwise, it is imperative that this group of people cannot be overlooked.

It is against this backdrop that the book, **LET'S REASON TOGETHER – YOUTH'S A-Z** is a timely one that is set to address the various issues that affect young people as well as their vision and aspirations. Since the primary goal of young people is to live full lives in their societies, this book examines specific elements that would help them in this process. It covers a wide range of issues from the sublime such as attitude, choices, education, health and xenophobia to the seemingly mundane such as dreams, integrity and vacation etc.

Oluwakemi Ola-Ojo has written from her wealth of experience both in the medical field as well as from a spiritual point of view and it is evident that a lot of research work was put into writing this book. Irrespective of your age and/or religious persuasion, this book will inform and guide you.

Book details:
Paperback: 316 pages
Language English
ISBN 978-0-9557898-7-8

Reviews
This is the most wonderful piece of youth work I have ever seen, capturing diverse situations and circumstances peculiar to youths. The work is thorough, educative and spiritually exhilarating. It is a must have for every youth worker to use, either in group discussions,

 :www.protokospublishers.com

OTHER BOOKS

seminars or straightforward teaching. This piece of work will yet raise the gospel abroad.
Dr M Akindele, Consultant Paediatrician, London, UK

This is a must read for the youths and anyone that deals with teenagers. All Sunday school staff will benefit from this book.
Deaconess B. Josiah. London, UK

COMING OUT SOON

- GOOD DADS, BAD DADS.
- INSPIRATIONS FOR THE MAN OF VALOUR.
- INSPIRATIONS FOR THE MAN OF COURAGE.
- MY A.B.C. OF PEOPLE AND THINGS IN THE BIBLE.

USEFUL ADDRESSES & WEBSITES

Care for the Family
PO Box 488
Cardiff
CF15 7YY
Tel: (029) 2081 0800
Fax: (029) 2081 4089
Email: mail@cff.org.uk
Website: www.care-for-the-family.org.uk OR www.cff.org.uk
Care for the Family aims to promote strong family life and to help those hurting because of family breakdown. Their heart is to come alongside people in the good times and in the tough times – bringing hope, compassion and some practical, down-to-earth help and encouragement.

Children Evangelism Ministry Inc
P.O. Box 4480
Ilorin, Kwara State,
Nigeria.
Tel: +234 31 222199
E-mail: cem@ilorin.skannet.com OR cem562000@yahoo.com
Children Evangelism Ministry Inc is a ministry that reaches out with the Gospel to children before and after birth. The ministry teaches and equips parents, teachers and coordinators of Sunday Schools and Children's Clubs. They also have and hold Children's Clubs, conferences and training seminars.

Focus on the Family
Tel: 1-800 - 232 6459
Website: www.family.org
Focus on the Family cooperates with the Holy Spirit in disseminating the Gospel of Jesus Christ to as many people as possible, and, specifically, to accomplish that objective by helping to preserve traditional values and the institution of the family.

Open Gate
2 Union Road
Croydon
CRO 2XU.
Tel: 0208 665 5533
Fax: 0208 684 7233
e-mail: opengate@yahoo.co.uk
   alteschool@yahoo.co.uk
Open Gate Provides a preventative and supplementary educational facility for youths at risk of permanent exclusion. We aim at empowering and connecting the youths for the future. We provide support for the family and the community.

Protokos Publishers
P.O. Box 48424
London
SE15 2YL
www.protokospublishers.com
Protokos Publishers provides various resources for the family. We publish many life's enlightening, informative and motivational must read books. With each of our books, you are guaranteed a 24/7 counsellor by your side on the subject.

The Shepherd's Ministries
5 Brookehowse Road
Bellingham
London SE6 3TJ, UK
Tel/Fax: +44 208 698 7222
Email: info@theshepherdsministries.org
Website: www.theshepherdsministries.org
The Shepherd's Ministries helps to bring children into an experience of worshipping God in truth and in spirit; give children a world-view based on God's word and mission and helps children to exercise their gifts in local and global missions.

'Let's Reason Together ...Youths' A-Z

Teenagers' Outreach Ministries (TOM) Inc.
Plot 85
Ladi Kwali Ext. Layout,
P.O.Box 16
Kwali, Abuja.
Nigeria.
Tel- 02082933730
Fax-02082933731
Nigeria - 08037044195, 07081860407
Email- tominthq@yahoo.co.uk
Website -www.tominternational.org
The Teenagers' Outreach Ministries (TOM) Inc. has a vision of leading today's teenager to Christ. This forms the foundation on which we mould their character in line with the word of God, thereby equipping them to fulfil their God ordained roles in life.

Total Woman Ministries
The Total Woman Ministries,
3 Herringham Road
Thames Wharf Barrier,
Charlton,
London
SE7 8NJ.
Tel: 020 8293 3730
Fax: 020 8293 3731
Email: admin@totalwomanministries.org
Website:www.totalwomanministries.org
Total Woman Ministries by God's grace has the sole vision of reaching out to women of all categories *(married, single, separated, divorced, young, middle-aged or elderly).*

United Christian Broadcasting UCB
P.O. Box 255, Stoke on Trent,
ST4 8YY, England
Among other forms of spreading the Gospel, UCB prints The Word For Today – a free daily devotional reading available for residents in the UK and Republic of Ireland

IN USA:
www.eCounseling.com
Tel Number: 1-866-268-6735

Dear Reader,

Thank you for your time and resources committed to supporting this writing ministry. Please help to tell others about how much the Lord has blessed you reading this book.

You will certainly be blessed by the other books written by Oluwakemi, so why not visit www.protokospublishers.com and place an order today.

It will equally be appreciated if you can help to write a few sentences review of the book on www.amazon.com and / or on www.protokospublishers.com.

Please note that all our books are easily available on our website and other good bookshops.

God bless you as you do.
Management
Protokos Publishers.

www.ingramcontent.com/pod-product-compliance
Lightning Source LLC
Chambersburg PA
CBHW051419290426
44109CB00016B/1357